THE END TIMES SIMPLIFIED

An overview of how the last days of human history may unfold

A J Ballinger

Andy,

enjoy during your

recovery. Tony

23/12/18

Text © A J Ballinger 2018

Printed by IngramSpark

ISBN 978-1-527233-07-2

British Library Cataloguing-in-Publication Data

A catalogue record for this book is available from the British Library

Contents

Foreword   5

A brief overview   6

Chapter 1   Where do we start?   8

    Enter the spiritual dimension   11

    A brief family tree   12

    The tents of Edom – most probably the Palestinians.   13

    Lot's two sons   14

    The Ishmaelites and Hagarites   15

    Amalek   15

    Assyria   15

    Well, why is Israel so important?   17

Chapter 2   The Coming War   19

    The Muslims   20

Chapter 3   The future months and years to the end   23

    a) The Psalm 83 war   23

    b) The Ezekiel 38 war   28

    Ezekiel 38/39   30

    Judgment on Gog   31

    Further notes on Ezekiel 38 and the Gog/Magog 'wars'.   32

    c) Isaiah 66: 6-8   33

    d) Matthew 24:34   33

    e) Daniel's 70 weeks prophecy   33

Chapter 4   The Rapture   41

Chapter 5   The Antichrist   46

Chapter 6   The 7 year Tribulation – also known as Daniel's 70th week   52

    a) The first three and a half years after the Ezekiel 38 'war'   52

    b) The Great Tribulation

Chapter 7   The book of Revelation simplified   77

Chapter 8   The Battle of Armageddon – an overview   97

Chapter 9   Questions answered   102

    a) Where is the Church during the Tribulation?   102

    b) Marriage of the Church   103

    c) The Millennial Kingdom   104

d) The very last days   105

e) The New Jerusalem   106

f) Resurrections and allocated living places   107

Chapter 10   Current events that have led up to the Ezekiel nations coming together for war with Israel   110

President Obama   112

The other half of Mr Obama   114

Back To Events That Transpired Under Obama's Rule   116

The mainstream media, fake news and false flags   118

President Trump   119

Why does this matter?   122

Enter Donald Trump   123

Trump   124

Trump's foreign policy in more detail   129

Nato   130

Iran   130

Turkey   130

Saudi Arabia   131

Russia.   131

China   131

A thought about Trump   132

Satan's ingress into the Church   132

The Luciferian Doctrine, Technology, UFOs and other nasties   133

What has this got to do with the End Times?   135

Final say   135

Foreword

Like every other person on Earth I want to know where I came from, why I am here and where I am going when I die.

Those questions were answered when I accepted Jesus Christ as my Saviour.

However, I remain on Earth and live amongst humanity, wondering how this planet will come to an end and the manner in which it will do so.

This has led me to a quest to know how the last days of humanity will unfold. There are obviously many religions, philosophers and wise men that have predicted the end of days according to their mindset and viewpoint of life but for the purposes of this book, it will come from the Jewish and Christian perspective. The reason I do this is that the Bible is unsurpassed in prophetic detail and accuracy, more so than any other book or combinations of books anywhere on Earth. No part of it has ever been disproved and countless prophecies in it have come to pass, dead on time. Many dissenters have come to know Christ as their Saviour by trying to prove its content wrong.

That is good enough for me.

You will see from this foreword, that I am intentionally making this book easy to understand so that the average person on the street can read what I have to say and weigh the evidence in their own time. I will not fall into the trap of giving you a complicated presentation that baffles all but the very intelligent, so this really is a story, *simplified*.

A brief overview

From the Jewish and Christian perspective, God made mankind and made 'him' (both male and female) to live on this Earth in harmony with Him and nature in a gorgeous place called the Garden of Eden. He made Adam first and from his one rib, made Eve. It's important to accept this literally happened and that the Bible is to be taken literally unless a verse or scripture makes it impossible to do so. Interpreting the Bible literally is called exegesis and is, in my opinion, the correct way to read God's written Word.

Eve was tempted into having more knowledge about 'everything' by Satan, who came in the symbolic form of a snake and the knowledge she desired came in the symbolic form of an apple, from which she ate. Sin entered humanity the moment Eve bit it and mankind was instantly severed from God's intimate presence. Adam and Eve lost their innocence and suddenly discovered they had been naked in the Garden (Genesis 3:7). Only a law of some kind would make them aware of this. It became the 'law of death'.

This act by Eve is evidence that women can sometimes be more easily led into deception than men, as she took the apple of knowledge while Adam did not, initially, but Adam is not to be let off lightly either. He was supposed to be Eve's 'head', covering her and protecting her from deception and evil and in this task he failed miserably. I can safely say, therefore, that Adam is equally, if not more so, to blame for the fall of mankind.

And so we arrive at the starting blocks of human history, where humanism and every religion finds us; separated from God. Some will want to be with God while others will revile Him until the day they die.

Some religions want to make us gods and others say we have to live this life a few gazillion times to get our act together and become like Him. Still others say we have to conquer other people and blow them up, to get to Heaven. But Christ's way is so simple. He simply says, 'Believe in me with all your heart, confess it with your mouth and you are saved' [paraphrased]. This statement is so simple that it has confounded mankind for centuries, including Christians who have added so much legalism and tradition to this simple truth that it has almost drowned it out. Christ's offer of salvation requires no self-flagellation (whipping), acting good or doing endless good works (although as you take on Christ's character you desire to do good works). All you have to do is believe that Christ is your Saviour. Period.

The Jews of course are still waiting for their Messiah and so are the Muslims. In fact whether you are a Bhuddist or believe in reincarnation you are still waiting for something to happen. Not so with Christianity, as our Saviour met with us two thousand years ago. Christians have more than left those starting blocks I talked about earlier; they have finished the race, by God's grace alone.

There are very few if any writings in Islam, Bhuddism, Hinduism or the secular world that predict with any clarity or accuracy how we will get back together with God or how the events in this world will unfold until we meet with God one day.

The Bible, however, is awash with prophecies and detail about 'the end times' and it is to this wonderful and rich source, that I now turn.

Chapter 1

Where do we start?

I have had a profound interest in the end times for over twenty five years but it is only in the last six years that my interest has become a study.

In my quest for understanding, I have read so many commentaries, that far from getting a satisfying answer, I became more and more confused. So I decided to turn to the Bible for help. But where does one start? It is a massive book, written (with God's guidance) by many human hands and contains dozens and dozens of prophesies of all kinds, with some apparently contradicting each other.

To answer my own question, one must first accept that the Bible is the inspired word of God and that its content is truth, that there are no fables or myths in it and that God's intention in giving us the Bible is for it to act as a roadmap back to Him. It is a Satnav to salvation!

Accepting this premise with an unsaved mind is very difficult and some readers may have even thrown this booklet away by now but I encourage you to persist with what I am saying here.

It is not enough to read the Bible with human eyes and try and understand what it means. A lack of belief in The One Who wrote the Bible will make it dead to your eyes. I know this for a fact because I used to read the Bible before I got saved and I found it weird, contradictory and definitely a book full of myths and fantasies. But when I got saved God did something wonderful to me, He took the scales off my eyes and I could understand the Bible. My spirit was now connected back to His like some form of power conduit. No computer works without a power cable so why should the Bible! This 'understanding' comes in the form of an utterance to me from God, called Rhema. Rhema literally means 'an utterance'.

However, even with God's Rhema opening up the scriptures of the Bible, I found myself like a baby in a milk factory. Where do I go and what do I do to get started? How do I discover, from all this wealth of truth, how mankind will develop and eventually come to an end on planet Earth.

Like a good computer, you have to press the start button to get it going, so that's what I did. I started reading from Genesis chapter 1.

WHERE DO WE START?

It didn't take me very long to realize that as mankind's journey down history started, a very early split in the human family tree occurred, which will have and is still having, a profound effect on the days that we are living in. So profound in fact that the split in this family will lead to the return of Christ during His second coming and the end of human history as we know it.

I am not talking about families wandering off into the unknown world from when Noah's Ark finally came to rest on solid ground, but I am talking about a very specific family and that is the family of Abraham.

Abraham is the father (literally) of the world's three monotheistic religions (that being a religion whose followers believe there is only one God). These religions are Judaism, Christianity and Islam. Their numbers make up a huge chunk of humanity.

God had a special plan for Abraham, for him to be the father of many nations and many peoples and kings (Genesis 15:5). God also went on to make a statement so profound that it is shaking the Earth to this day, that Abraham's descendants would occupy all land from Egypt to the river Euphrates (Genesis 15: 18-21) and would do so under a covenant. A covenant (a pledge or a promise) from God is something that cannot be broken.

Now, Abram (high, exalted father) who would become Abraham (father of a multitude) was confused how he would become the father of many nations, as he was an old man, about 85 years of age when he was given this news and was childless to boot. But God nonetheless promised Abram that he would be the father of many peoples (Genesis15:5) and in this Abram trusted Him implicitly (Genesis 15:6).

Abram must have told his wife Sarai about this message from God, that he would be the father of many nations. However, as I mentioned earlier, some women are more easily led astray than men and there is little doubt that at this point Sarai reminded Abram that she was infertile or restrained from having a child (Genesis 16 : 2). So she made an alternative suggestion that instead of offspring coming through her, that Abram would have children through Hagar, their Egyptian maid. This was common practice in those days, when the inability to produce an heir was unacceptable.

The decision by Sarai to let her husband Abram have a child with Hagar is undoubtedly the most dangerous decision to have been made since Eve's rebellious act in the Garden of Eden, to this very day, for through that decision the enemies of Israel and God were brought into fruition in human vessels. Who knows what would have happened if there had never been a Hagar, whose descendants have spawned the Muslim hordes now facing down Judaism and Christianity all over the world?

Hagar gave a son to Abram and he was called Ishmael (God hears – Genesis 16:11) and when Hagar knew she was pregnant she became full of contempt for Sarai and despised her (Genesis 16: 4).

Even in the womb, the father of the Semetic Arabian peoples, Ishmael (all descendants from Shem, one of the sons of Noah, are S[h]emetic people) despised the "Princess" of the Jews, Sarai and her descendants (Sarai was to be called Sarah, which means 'Princess'). The descendants of 'Princess' Sarah of course are the (Semetic) Jews (a name derived from Judah).

And so a conflict that we see on our television screens every night, was born, the conflict between the Semetic Arabs and the (Semetic) Jews (plus a whole load of other people that are not originally Semetic at all). This family feud has been going on since Abraham's day and will culminate in the return of Christ and the end of days; but more about that later.

The animosity between Sarai and Hagar got so bad that Sarai told Abram of her discontent (Genesis 16:5). Abram replied by saying that Hagar was under Sarai's power and must do Sarai's bidding. (Genesis 16:6).

Sarai took advantage of her power over Hagar and treated her very badly, to the extent that she ran way. She was found by an Angel of the Lord (actually God Himself) at a well (Genesis 16:7). It was at this well that Hagar was told that her son would be a "wild ass" of a man, named Ishmael (Genesis 16: 11-12) and that he would live to the east of his kinsmen. This is a very important scripture, as we shall see later.

Abram was 86 years old when Hagar gave birth and Sarai was 76. We do not know how old Hagar was. It intrigues me, however, that when Abram originally left his ancestral homeland, Haran, at the age of 75, he eventually entered Egypt to buy food (in the midst of a drought) but was fearful that his beautiful wife Sarai (Genesis 12:11) would cause him to be killed when a jealous Egyptian saw her. To overcome this threat, Abram called Sarai his sister and due to her being "single" in the eyes of the Egyptians and very beautiful, was offered to Pharaoh's harem. This enabled Abram to become very wealthy because the Pharaoh showered goods on him, because his 'sister' was so beautiful. It also intrigues me that God kept Sarai barren in the harem, to prevent Israel's Princess getting pregnant no doubt.

Well, has anyone done the math yet? Sarai was 66 years of age when she entered that harem and that should be good news for all our ladies!

That is by the way, so back to our historical analysis. About fourteen years after Ishmael was born, Sarai gave birth to Isaac and so Sarai's name changed to Sarah and Abram became Abraham. Isaac's name means 'laughter'.

Abraham threw a great feast; the same day Isaac was weaned (Genesis 21:8). It was about this time that Sarah saw Ishmael mocking Isaac (Genesis 21:9). Sarah was so annoyed she asked Abraham to cast Hagar and Ishmael out of their camp and this caused great pain and anxiety for Abraham, as he dearly loved Ishmael (Genesis 21:11).

What God said next is absolutely profound and has not only resulted in years of war but would also culminate in our Saviour arriving safely on Earth to deliver us from the hell that is to come. He chose Isaac as Abraham's heir, even though Ishmael was his first-born son! (Genesis 17:21) Well who cares, some would say. Why is this so important? Why is this so important? Because not only was it unheard of to have a younger son named as an heir, it led to hatred towards Isaac's descendants, in the hearts of Ishmael's descendants, to this day. The very Palestinian conflict we see today, started here.

Remember, if we take the Bible literally, God gave all the land from the Nile river in Egypt to the Euphrates river to Isaac and his descendants and that geographical area is roughly the size Israel will become during the Millennium. More on this later though.

Enter the spiritual dimension

If we decide that the modern day conflict in the middle east is purely over land and that there is no spiritual aspect to the conflict then you may as well use this book as a firelighter or go and prune your roses.

The central theme of the conflict is spiritual and not territorial. This is something very few secular people accept or realize, especially the liberal mainstream media in the west.

Some contemporary scholars like Norman Finkelstein will tell you that if the Jews ceded east Jerusalem to the Palestinians and withdrew from the west bank, there would be peace eternal and every Muslim on Earth would smile and put down his weapon.

Yasser Arafat was offered just such a deal in 1993, as part of the Oslo peace accords. However, Yasser Arafat and his cohorts knew that accepting such a deal would end the billions in aid that he and his henchmen were spiriting away to Swiss bank accounts and to boot, Israel would still be alive, festering in their neighbourhood. So he squandered a real opportunity for a 'Palestinian' homeland, allowing terrorism to thrive under the protective, one-sided agreement and that same terrorism festers to this day.

It is a central tenet of Islam that any territory that was once owned by Muslims must return to them, if taken in battle. We all know that Muslims through the ages have fought and lost and then won what was called Canaan on many occasions and through the Ottoman Empire, governed 'Palestine' for centuries. To the Muslim mindset, 'Palestine' is theirs and they have a rightful claim to it.

That is a territorial claim that is based on a human perspective. However, we need to be reminded of the spiritual perspective of God having said that the seed of Abraham (via Isaac) would own that land, even from the Nile river to the Euphrates. How many Jewish and Christian scholars, over the centuries, when Israel was in exile, must have thought that the Lord got it wrong, that Genesis 15:18 was an error or that His promise only lasted a short while before being broken?

Remember, if we believe in God and take His promises literally, then the land mentioned in Genesis 15:18 will one day become Israel and will remain Israel until God destroys planet Earth in a ball of fire. Does this sound like a human promise or one from God? If you accept it is from God then this is a spiritual battle, and not a human one that is being fought over territory. As 'Greater Israel' does not yet exist and indeed if the world had its way, would perish altogether, how will this promise be fulfilled?

To answer this question, we need to understand who the people are that are living in 'Palestine', who their neighbours are and why they want Israel out of the way. In order to do this we need to establish the ancient family names of the people currently showing such an avid interest in the destruction of Israel and where they currently live. The overview in the following pages is very simple, as we need to focus on current events in more detail later on.

A brief family tree

From the Jewish perspective, Abraham's seed (via Isaac) resulted in twelve tribes that settled in areas of modern day Israel, parts of Syria, Iraq, Jordan and the Negev. (This sounds remarkably like Genesis 15:18 not so?). Dan settled in the north with Simeon in the south. (It is recommended you look at a map of Israel showing where the twelve tribes settled to understand this better).

From the Muslim perspective (remember these people only slowly started becoming Muslim from the 6th century onwards) the ancient nations that settled in and around Israel look something like this:

Tents of Edom – descendants of Esau – Palestinians living in west bank, Gaza, Lebanon and Jordan.

Ishmaelites – Arabs to the east of Israel

Moab – central Jordan. Moab was an illegitimate son of Lot (Genesis 19: 36-38). Lot was the nephew of Abraham and settled to the east of Abraham's territory.

Hagarites – clan of Ishmaelites – do not mistake them for Egyptians because Hagar was Egyptian. The Hagarites were called the Gerrheans by the Greeks and lived to the east Gilead (this is important to remember when we discuss the war alluded to in Psalm 83).

Ammon – northen Jordan. Another illegitimate son of Lot.

Amalek – South Jordan

Philistia – Gaza.

Assyria – Syria/Western Iraq.

Lebanon proper – Phoenecian peoples.

It may be obvious to the reader that we have already discussed some of the people in the list, above. But who are the other main players and how do we know who they are? As I have said already, the Bible is faultless in letting us know.

Let's look at a few of the main players, in the list of peoples shown above.

The tents of Edom – most probably the Palestinians.

Esau was the brother of Jacob, one of the sons of Isaac. It is reported that even in their mother's womb, the two struggled with each other (Genesis 25:22). Esau was the elder brother and should have received Isaacs blessing to be his heir, but he was cheated out of this inheritance over a bowl of gruel and Isaac's blessing went to Jacob instead and more importantly, the inheritance of all Isaac's land and future promises of land went with the blessing. This eventually caused Esau great anguish and he became very angry towards his brother. Do you see a common thread here? Hagar's son, Ishmael, also lost his inheritance to Isaac and Hagar remained embittered until her death.

Esau, an embittered man, decided not to marry any Jewish woman in Canaan and so turned to Ishmael's daughter, Mahalath and married her instead. This meant that the bitterness towards Abraham and Isaac, in the heart of Hagar, flowed through to the hatred of Jacob at the hands of Esau. One could almost imagine Esau and a very old Hagar sitting around a camp fire spewing jaundiced views About Abraham, Isaac and Jacob, the three Patriarchs of the Jewish people.

I am sure some of this must have rubbed of on their combined descendants. An animosity for the seed of Isaac and Jacob had been born and exists to this very day.

Esau eventually formed the Kingdom of Edom and his descendants warred with Israel for many years, eventually losing a lot of power and parts of their land. They continue to do so today under their modern name of 'Palestinians'. The book of Obadiah and Psalm 83: 6 makes it very clear that Edom became the 'Palestinians', more commonly known as the tent dwellers. Their bloodline is mixed with the Philistines and the terrible Herodian lineage came from them too. They cheered when the Babylonians took the Jews into captivity. The very same people continue to agitate and show hatred towards Israel to this very day.

Lot's two sons

As I have mentioned, Lot was Abraham's nephew. When he left the land of his ancestors with Abraham, he initially settled with Abraham in the land of Canaan but soon friction arose because there was not enough grazing land for the large number of people that moved with Abraham and the herdsmen of the two men bickered over grazing rights. In the end Abraham suggested to Lot to move to an area of his own choice. Abraham said to Lot, 'if you go west I will go east and if you go east, I will go west'.

Lot looked east to the Jordan valley which was very lush and beautiful in that day and went to settle there (Genesis 13:11). The cities in that part of the world were filled with exceedingly vicious and violent men and it was not long before God destroyed the cities by raining brimstone down on them. Lot and his family were spared by God, but Lot's wife craved the lifestyle there and looking back on the city of Sodom, was turned into a pillar of salt. God had commanded that none of them should look back lest they turn to salt. It's interesting to note that the area where Sodom was built, is to this day covered in large quantities of salt and round balls of fossilized brimstone (Sulphur).

Lot was now without a wife and he fled to the mountains to hide, with his daughters. It was important in those days that the family lineage should not perish and because there were no men for the daughters to have children with, they agreed to sleep with their father for their bloodline to continue. Two boys were born from these acts, one to each sister, the one being called Moab and the other called Ammon. They settled in the North and central parts of Jordan.

The purpose of this book is not to go into too much detail, but safe to say that the Moabites and Ammonites became enemies of Israel and often fought with them. This can be studied further in the book of Exodus and Judges, at your own leisure.

So we have a second branch of a family tree that turned against the descendents of Isaac and Jacob.

The Ishmaelites and Hagarites

From earlier notes you will see that these are tribes that descended from Ishmael (and possibly) Hagar and they were later to become the Arabic peoples that live in modern day Iraq, Saudi Arabia and the Arab peninsular. It should be plain, by now, to see they were also enemies of Israel due to the split that happened with Abraham and Isaac.

Some scholars claim that this group of people are the ancient ancestors of the prophet Mohammed but unlike the Bible, Islamic records are not clear enough to record genealogy accurately. This is yet another branch of an ancient family tree that turned against their Jewish relatives.

Amalek

Amalek was the grandson of Esau who was in turn the eldest son of Isaac. We have already discussed how Esau turned against his relatives for being cheated out of Isaac's blessing and inheritance by Jacob and no doubt this seed of bitterness carried on into Amalek as he was a very strong leader among the Edomites who fought many battles with Israel, their nation eventually losing most of their power and land, being dispersed to the border regions of Judah's territory (now called Jordan).

Assyria

Assyria, which includes modern day Syria and north western Iraq, will play a major role in the soon coming war with Israel.

Assyria has an extremely rich history and boasts the oldest inhabited cities on Earth, had some of the best troops of all ages, was steeped in culture and the arts and fought many battles with its neighbours and other kingdoms. From Shalmaneser 3rd to Adad-Nirari 3rd, conquests of the Israelites took place in a flow and ebb of attacks and conquest, with parts of the Assyrian Empire belonging to greater Israel and then shrinking under Assyrian attack. The Assyrian Empire was one of the biggest in the history of the region, stretching from Georgia in southern Russia to the ends of Persia (Iran). The original inhabitants were Semetic (descended from Shem), as were the Israelites, and Ashur, the second son of Shem, who was the grandson of Noah, was reported to have built the magnificent city of

Nineveh. The name Assyria is largely attributed to the name of Ashur (the city of Assur was named after him).

It is worth noting that two of Ashur's brothers were called Aram and Elam, as they will play a role in understanding who it is that surrounds Israel to this day. A quick look at the family tree of Noah will clearly show who is who in his family tree and will help the reader to begin to understand who the people are that settled in the region and who they are in modern times.

From this brief, historical analysis, it is clear to see that modern day Israel is surrounded by a group of peoples who have been at war with her for millennia and continue to be either in a state of war or on the verge of war with her. It is worth remembering that many of these people are closely related to each other in terms of bloodline and in many respects the Middle East conflict is nothing more than a big family squabble with intense spiritual dimensions.

Well, this is not what the media and humanists point out. Instead they are constantly harping on about a struggle for land and the redress of wrongs and imbalances and oppression. But this is not the case and is the reason why I have said, from the very beginning of this book, that the struggle against Israel is not about land or a family argument, but rather it's a spiritual battle. The very core of the whole struggle against Israel, whether it be at the hands of the 'Palestinians' or the Syrians or the Egyptians or indeed the whole world, is a spiritual one, to cut off the Saviour's bloodline.

What do I mean by this? The answer is quite simple. The one bloodline that split off from Abraham led to Islam and the other led to Judaism and Christianity. The bloodline that ran down the centuries from Abraham, Isaac and Jacob led to the birth of mankind's saviour, Jesus Christ. The bloodline that went from Abraham through Ishmael, became a groupings of people who have fallen under the umbrella of Islam, a religious, political and spiritual movement that is directly opposed to the very existence of Judaism and Christianity. The Godhead of one group is opposed to the godhead of the other. This is therefore a spiritual battle. If we accept this conflict is indeed spiritual, then we can understand why the forces of darkness want to rid the world of Jews and Christians, as the latter's bloodline exalts the God of the universe.

Indeed, Satan tried his best to destroy the bloodline of the Jews before Christ and has tried to eliminate them ever since. He did it under the Romans, in the pogroms in Europe in the dark ages, in the reformation and in Hitler's death camps. But the self-same attacks are now being turned against Christians in high numbers, as we are seen as corporate enemies of the god of Islam. Every Muslim-dominant country like Egypt or Syria or Nigeria or Iraq is brutalizing and killing Christians in large numbers. Why would they be doing that if the issue was only over land?

If we accept, therefore, that the war between Jews/Christians and Islam is a spiritual war, then we can delve even deeper into the Bible to find out what lies in store for all of us called 'human'.

The entire conflict in the middle-east is where the forces of light and dark meet. I can say with total confidence that Israel is a light fighting ever growing forces of darkness, including many within the soon-to-diminish United States of America.

Well, why is Israel so important?

Israel is important because God made a covenant with the Jews that they will live in the land for all time and that its people will become like the grains of sand on the seashore, eventually filling out most of Egypt, Jordan, Lebanon and Syria/Iraq in the millennium.

Satan, who is jealous of God, has decided to wipe out the Jews for one main reason. If he can eliminate the Jews then God's covenant with the Jews will be broken and if the covenant is broken, then God is a liar and if God is a liar, he does not exist. If God does not exist, then the antithesis of God can rule, namely Satan himself. This is the age-old desire of Satan, to usurp God's role as THE God of the universe. Satan has therefore taken hold of this ancient feud between Israel and her neighbours (and soon the whole world) to bring God down from His throne once and for all; by "simply" eliminating Israel.

Now you know why one of the most inventive, creative, wealthy, intelligent, humanistic, compassionate races the world has ever seen, has been (for millennia), ostracised, killed, attacked, slandered, dispossessed, gassed and disenfranchised! Just for being Jewish? Now you know why there is hatred in nearly all of the world's media for these gallant people – it is spiritual! It is because, whether we like it or not, the Jews are the 'apple of God's eye', the 'apple' being the very centre of the eye.

Why are Jews hounded and pressured the way they are when they have given more to the world in science and art than any other race on Earth? With over 250 Nobel prize-winners among them. Is this how the world should thank them? Why is such a tiny little piece of land called the 'west bank' so important to the world that it would go to nuclear war over it, which is something that may very well happen, if there is no spiritual dimension to this conflict? Would the world go to war if North Sudan conquered South Sudan? Not likely! Or maybe if the dispute over the Falkland Islands flared up again? Impossible!

The land of Israel is at the forefront of the war between Heaven and Hell and it is from that tiny land mass, which is hundreds of times smaller than the surrounding Arabic land, that wars, tribulation and the extinction of the unbelieving human being will spring forth. It is around the borders of that speck of land that great armies will perish and from whence its protector will issue forth earthquakes of mind-boggling proportions to keep the 'apple of His eye' safe.

No empire has ever defeated Israel; yes, some may have delayed its safe dwelling in the land, but more often than not God allowed this during times of rebellion by His people, so as to chastise them. The longest chastisement of the Jews started when Christ was hung on the cross, as it was then that the Jews rejected their saviour and so for two millennia they wandered in and out of alien countries before God called them home. The calling home of the Jews to Israel was prophesied in Ezekiel 20:34 and Isaiah 11:11-12 (among many other similar prophecies) and that in itself is a two-fold miracle; the first being that such old prophecies were uttered and the second miracle that it came to pass, offering Israel a re-birthed homeland in one day in1948 (Isaiah 66:8). Fine examples of how incredibly accurate the Bible is.

It is hopefully known to the reader that the Israelites fought many hundreds of battles to defend their homeland, which over the centuries was either larger or smaller than Israel's current land-mass. They won many battles, including some against awesome odds and while they lost many battles and were carried away into exile by both Assyria and Babylonia, they were never missing from the 'promised land' for long. Even after the Romans finally crushed the Jews in the second century AD, populations of Jews remained in what is called Israel today, with Judea and Samaria being key parts of their kingdom. Today Judea and Samaria are part of the 'west bank' of 'Palestine'.

It is therefore reasonable to assume that one of the best ways the enemy of Israel can remove her from the land, is by war. Not only would this break God's covenant but it would be the dream of every Muslim to take back land that they consider Islamic, since that is one of their prime directives in life, to never permanently surrender any land formerly occupied by Muslims, as indeed Israel was under the Ottoman empire and others before that. And any student of the Bible or even geopolitics will tell you that a war is brewing in the middle east, even as I type these words.

When will that war come and how can we look for it in the Bible? That is the topic of the next chapter.

Chapter 2
The Coming War

It's logical to any military historian and even to those with a bit of common sense, that any future war involving Israel will have to come through its borders. Even though we live in a day and age where vast numbers of troops can be dropped by air, the supporting logistics will require supply routes over land or from across the sea to various beach-heads. None of Israel's immediate neighbours have the wealth or military power to invade Israel from the air or from the sea. The only remaining entry route, therefore is by land.

This is precisely why the enemies of Israel want the west bank to become a Palestinian state; not so much as to offer the 'Palestinians' a homeland, but to ensure that the borders of Israel will remain indefensible. For, without the high Golan heights and the dividing depths of the River Jordan's valley, through which only a handful of roads pass, Israel would be defenceless. Indeed, in some sections, Israel would only be ten miles wide and a quick thrust at this narrow point by a determined enemy, would cut Israel in half and with it, all military supply routes from the north to the south. It would be the death of Israel.

Remember, this is a spiritual battle and the forces of darkness want the Jews as an entire race of people to be eliminated. Words to this effect have been broadcast far and wide from Iran, to Syria to Hamas and Hezbollah. None of these fanatics want peace with Israel under any circumstances and some quotes I have read recently indicate that the surrender of Israel would not be enough for peace, but only the total elimination of Jews as a race would suffice. There can be no other explanation than the spiritual dimension to foster this hatred.

Jews may have brought a lot of their fate upon themselves, by denying Christ and accepting that His death would be on the shoulders of following Jewish generations and indeed the death camps of Auschwitz, the progroms of Europe and the reformation are stark testimony to the fact that God gave to the Jews what they asked for ... punishment, for denying their Jewish Saviour Jesus.

Satan would now like to drive a stake into the heart of the 'Apple of God's eye' by eliminating the Jews altogether, thus ridding himself of a people he detests and if succeeding in doing so, the elimination of God Himself. For God will be a liar if the Jews disappear and if He is a liar, He does not exist!

This my friends, is just how serious the situation in the middle east is. It is the focal point of the war between light and dark, between Heaven and hell.

The Muslims

I am not going to bore the reader with endless pages describing how Islam arose and what it stands for. You can study that separately if you wish. However, the place of the Muslim hordes in the end days of humanity is key to what happens to humanity.

In a nutshell, Islam was founded by Mohammed, who having seen and heard from 'angelic' forces (particularly 'Gabriel'), decided to preach what he was hearing. His own writings plus the writings of others close to him, known as Hadiths, basically formed the Koran as we know it today. You may have noticed that I put the words 'angelic' and 'Gabriel' in inverted commas. The reason I did this is because I do not believe that the angelic beings that visited Mohammed were from God but were demonic usurpers. I say this because the Koran is diametrically opposed to Judeo-Christian teachings and so it stands to reason that the real Gabriel would not give a revelation to Muslims that contradicted Jewish and Christian writings. It is a vast subject in itself but basically, Satan has tried to emulate God's plan from time immemorial and often 'duplicates' events and writings that come from the Judeo-Christian God. Remember, the authors of the Koran had many hundreds of years to read Jewish and Christian scripture but it is only when Mohammed turned against the Jews that writings against Judaism sprang forth with all their hatred:-

Q. 5:60 Say (O Muhammad to the people of the Scripture [Jews]): 'Shall I inform you of something worse than that, regarding the recompense from Allah: those (Jews) who incurred the Curse of Allah and His Wrath, those of whom (some) He transformed into monkeys and swines, those who worshipped Taghut (false deities); such are worse in rank (on the Day of Resurrection in the Hellfire), and far more astray from the Right Path.'

This is further evidence that the war of hatred against Israel is spiritual, for it is found in the pages of the fiercest religion on Earth, from the very Muslim holy book itself! So for apologists like Chomsky and Finkelstein to write off the spiritual aspect of this war, is in my mind, complete folly. It is the ONLY reason for the conflict.

When Mohammed died, his successors started to squabble about who should succeed him. One group said it should be his descendants while the other said it should be an elected man. The group that chose the descendants became known as Shia Muslims (as only God can choose a successor) while those who advocated election from the community became known as Sunni Muslims. The split became so severe that Sunni and Shia Muslims have been fighting each other for centuries; the end goal of both being a Muslim caliphate that will rule the world under their Mhadi. However, the Shia Muslims believe it will be their 12th Imam Mohammed al-Mhadi that will rule and that he is alive, waiting in a state of occultation and the Sunnis believe he will be an elected ruler that has descended from Mohammed himself and will be called Mohammed (how they will know he is a descendant is unclear as the Koran's genealogy is very poor). It is a great blessing to Israel that Islam's house is divided as they have been killing each other since the 6th century. It has resulted in in a lot of energy, money and power being expended fighting each other rather than their common enemy, the Jews and on an increasing scale, Christians too. Their division will, I believe, also play a part in the battle of Ezekiel in years to come, when Israel's enemies turn on each other. I foresee Sunni and Shia attacking each other as they march on Jerusalem.

Coming back to the peoples that surround modern-day Israel, we now know who they are in ancestral terms but now we need to know who they are in the pecking order of Islam. The following list will give you an idea:

Egypt – large Sunni majority
Jordan – large Sunni majority
Lebanon – 27% Sunni with large Christian and Shia populations, the latter mainly Hezbollah.
Syria – large Sunni majority with Alawite minority as ruling party. The Alawites align themselves with Shia Islam.
Iraq – large Shia majority
Iran – A very large Shia majority
Qatar – a ruling Sunni minority among a Shia majority.
Turkey – Sunni majority
Saudi Arabia – A very large Sunni majority
Yemen – Sunni majority.
Sunnis make up about 85% of the world's Muslim population.

If you look at a map of the middle east and slide the Sunni/Shia label onto them you will very quickly see that the nations to the north of Israel are mainly Shia (north in the Biblical sense included Syria, Iraq and Iran as invasions always came from the northern trade routes).

Although the pro-Shia Alawites in Syria are under strain to survive, they nonetheless form part of a Shia arc of nations across the northern section of Israel. The southern arc, namely Egypt, Yemen, Saudi Arabia and Qatar are made up of Sunnis. This sounds very similar to the 'kings of the north' and 'kings of the south' that will invade Israel after the Antichrist sets himself up in Jerusalem; but more of that later.

Before I go into identifying which countries will go to war with Israel and in what order, I need to briefly side-track back to Islam.

Please study it for yourself, but in the Shia belief system, the Imam that will rule in the last days of history is their 12th Imam. By studying who he is, you will see that he is currently living in a well in a state of minor occultation, having fallen in there as a boy. He did not die and is waiting to be resurrected, into a state of higher occultation. In the meantime he is communicating with Shia Muslims through holy men, the most revered of whom is the Ayatollah. This gives the Ayatollah unprecedented power over Shia Muslims and explains why Iranian leaders always defer to the Ayatollah when political decisions are made.

It is from this hellish state that so much hatred spews out against Israel. In fact, according to various Hadiths (teachings) the 12th Imam cannot rule the world until:

a) Israel is destroyed
b) there is unlimited chaos on the Earth.

He will then come alive and defeat all the nations of the world alongside Jesus (of all people!). You see how Islamic writings have taken Godly scriptures and real people from the Judeo-Christian perspective and twisted them horribly, counterfeiting all that the true God says will happen. In a sense, the Shia Imam will be the equivalent of our Christ and this further demonstrates how Satan has used Islamic teachings to his advantage.

Now you know why Iran is building a nuclear device in North Korea and fomenting so much terrorism in the world, it is their chief goal; to bring their saviour out of the well and onto the throne.

Chapter 3

The future months and years to the end

There are five scriptures that anchor the coming wars to a fixed point in history, which in turn fix the Rapture and the coming of the Antichrist. These in turn fix the timing of the Tribulation and the Second Coming of Christ.

The five scriptures are only five of many that help fix, in time, when the end time events will occur:

a) The war alluded to or prophesied in Psalm 83.
b) The Ezekiel 38 'war'.
c) Isaiah 66: 7-8
d) Matthew 24: 34
e) The 70 weeks prophecy in the book of Daniel 9: 24-27

a) The Psalm 83 war

There are many scriptures that talk about war with Israel, but all of them except a few that prophecy the coming Wars of Ezekiel 38, the wars against the Antichrist and the battle of Armageddon, are all to do with past wars in Israel's very long history.

There is one war however, that is not a war in the past, nor a direct prophecy of one in the future, but rather a future war that is *alluded to*. This is found in Psalm 83. The future war that this Psalm alludes to may well have taken place in the 1967 war with Israel, but it is the end of the Psalm that indicates the countries that fight in this future war will no longer exist as separate entities.

To understand what I am talking about, you must read the entire Psalm, as follows:

New King James:
A Song. A Psalm of Asaph.

83 Do not keep silent, O God!

Do not hold Your peace,
And do not be still, O God!
[2] For behold, Your enemies make a tumult;
And those who hate You have lifted up their head.
[3] They have taken crafty counsel against Your people,
And consulted together against Your sheltered ones.
[4] They have said, 'Come, and let us cut them off from *being* a nation,
That the name of Israel may be remembered no more.'
[5] For they have consulted together with one consent;
They form a confederacy against You:
[6] The tents of Edom and the Ishmaelites;
Moab and the Hagrites;
[7] Gebal, Ammon, and Amalek;
Philistia with the inhabitants of Tyre;
[8] Assyria also has joined with them;
They have helped the children of Lot. Selah
[9] Deal with them as *with* Midian,
As *with* Sisera,
As *with* Jabin at the Brook Kishon,
[10] Who perished at En Dor,
Who became *as* refuse on the Earth.
[11] Make their nobles like Oreb and like Zeeb,
Yes, all their princes like Zebah and Zalmunna,
[12] Who said, 'Let us take for ourselves
The pastures of God for a possession.'
[13] O my God, make them like the whirling dust,
Like the chaff before the wind!
[14] As the fire burns the woods,
And as the flame sets the mountains on fire,
[15] So pursue them with Your tempest,
And frighten them with Your storm.
[16] Fill their faces with shame,
That they may seek Your name, O Lord.
[17] Let them be confounded and dismayed forever;
Yes, let them be put to shame and perish,
[18] That they may know that You, whose name alone *is* the Lord,
Are the Most High over all the Earth.

This is a remarkable scripture not so? It not only lists the peoples that would want to form a confederacy against Israel, but they include many of the names of peoples and nations you are now familiar with. You can see this is not a direct prophecy, as it is a prayer to confound the success of a (future) confederacy warring against Israel, but the interesting thing is this confederacy has <u>never</u> come together as an entity that resulted in the participating nations *perishing*!

It seems logical then, that this event has not happened yet, as no past war fits its description . Yes, many of the nations listed, combined forces in the wars of 1948,1956,1967 and1973 to try and smash Israel, but all of those nations remain intact to this day. None of them have *perished*. Indeed, from the day that Psalm was written (looking forward) no confederacy of that description has fought Israel and perished. Not from David's times to the current day.

So why was Psalm 83 written? Why write about a confederacy that has not set foot on the world stage unless it is still meant to happen? It would be a waste of paper and ink otherwise!

To get to grips with what Psalm 83 says I need to break it down, segment by segment and give you a few pieces of analysis relating to its content and indeed, reading it as if it was being announced on television and radio waves in Israel today, really brings it alive.

A Song. A Psalm of Asaph. (*Italics by the author*)

83 Do not keep silent, O God!

Do not hold Your peace,

And do not be still, O God!

² For behold, Your enemies make a tumult; *[Is this not true today?]*

And those who hate You have lifted up their head.

³ They have taken crafty counsel against Your people,

And consulted together against Your sheltered ones. *[Aliyah-ed Jews? Jews escaping anti-Semitism?]*

⁴ They have said, 'Come, and let us cut them off from being a nation,

That the name of Israel may be remembered no more.' *[All past and present 'Palestinian' leaders continue to spew this almost word for word to this day]*

⁵ For they have consulted together with one consent;

They form a confederacy against You:

⁶ The tents of Edom *[Palestinians]* and the Ishmaelites *[Arabic nations]*;

Moab and the Hagrites; *[The Hagrites or Hagarites are not Egyptians. Some scholars believe that any of the major 20th century wars with Israel that included Egypt qualified said war as a type of Psalm 83 war but indeed the Hagarites lived east of Gilead. They were called the Gerrheans by the Greeks. Egypt had been around for millennia by the* time Psalm 83 was written and its people had always been called Egyptians, not Hagarites. *This simple understanding has stumped many Bible scholars into thinking a war related to Psalm 83 must have already happened as Egypt fought Israel many times. Discovering who the Hagarties actually were changes the whole concept of the Psalm 83 war to a futuristic one]*

7 Gebal ,*[Hezbollah]* Ammon [*Palestinians]*, and Amalek *[Nomadic Arabian peoples]*;

Philistia *[Gaza]* with the inhabitants of Tyre *[Lebanon]*;

8 Assyria also has joined with them *[Syria and western Iraq]*;

They have helped the children of Lot. Selah *[A regime change will have to take place in Jordan for Syria to help a Sunni country fight Israel, which is quite interesting]*.

9 Deal with them as *with* Midian *[The 4th son of Abraham through Keturah, a man who worshipped false gods]*,

As *with* Sisera, *[Canaanite General]*

As *with* Jabin at the Brook Kishon, *[A King of Canaan who opposed Joshua]*

10 Who perished at En Dor, [Canaanite city]

Who became *as* refuse on the Earth.

11 Make their nobles like Oreb and like Zeeb, *[Midianite Princes]*

Yes, all their princes like Zebah and Zalmunna, *[Midianite Kings Gideon beat]*

12 Who said, 'Let us take for ourselves

The pastures of God for a possession.'

13 O my God, make them like the whirling dust,

Like the chaff before the wind!

14 As the fire burns the woods,

And as the flame sets the mountains on fire,

15 So pursue them with Your tempest,

And frighten them with Your storm.

16 Fill their faces with shame,

That they may seek Your name, O Lord.

17 Let them be confounded and dismayed forever;

Yes, let them be put to shame and perish *[The countries and people listed above still exist today. This proves Psalm 83 has been written about a conflict that has still not happened, but will do so shortly. It also confirms that in the coming Psalm 83 war, the modern day nations surrounding Israel, or at least the radicals living in them, will PERISH FOREVER!],*

[18] That they may know that You, whose name alone is the Lord,
Are the Most High over all the Earth.

The war with the Mdianites (a war that foreshadows the Psalm 83 war)

To understand the full import of what the coming Psalm 83 war means to Israel, we need to understand who it was that fought the Midianites. After all, the Psalm describes the destruction of the Midianite peoples as a foreshadowing of the coming battle.

Although the Midianites were directly related to Abraham, they took the course of worshipping false gods and eventually became firm enemies of the Jews, harassing them, attacking them and taxing them to the point of destruction. The life of a Jew under the Midianite kings of the day was one of sheer oppression and ill treatment (sound familiar?).

No doubt God allowed this to happen as the Jewish people themselves had wandered from God and were in a state of rebellion. God often allowed His people to become oppressed so that they would cry out to Him for rescue and salvation, at which point He was often quick to respond. He was and is a jealous God and wants their undivided worship.

The man God raised to bring His people back to Him was Gideon and you can read about his exploits in the book of Judges.

Initially, Gideon raised an army of approximately 30 000 men to attack the Midianites but God wanted to show Gideon and His people that He, God Himself, would bring a crushing defeat upon the Midianites, which would bring them back to Him in worship.

To this end, and you all know the story of the golden fleece, God arranged that all but 300 men would go home and not join the battle. He did this by selecting only the men who drew water up to their mouths when drinking at a river, rather than those who put their mouths into the water and lapped it with their tongues. As a person interested in military affairs, I believe God chose those who brought the water to their mouths because you can remain alert in this stance, but not so with your face looking at water.

In any event, only 300 men attacked the massive Midianite army, confusing them to the point that they attacked each other, fleeing in terror while trumpets blasted. This is where parallels with the coming war start to take shape.

Conclusions we can draw from the Psalm 83 war

- It will involve military personnel who achieve a major victory against a fierce enemy, with supernatural help from the Lord.
- There will be confusion in the ranks of the enemy. (Sunni/Shia split?)
- The countries to be fought are the immediate neighbours of Israel or the radicals living in them.
- The defeat of the enemy will be so profound with such a high level of destruction that they will be ' confounded and dismayed forever'. To this end, they do not take part in the Ezekiel 38/39 war. The nations mentioned in Psalm 83 are missing from Ezekiel 38/39. But more of that to follow.

It is possible that Damascus will be destroyed in this battle (Isaiah 17 and Jeremiah 49) although the Ezekiel 38 'war' is more likely when the city will be destroyed. Verse 26 of Jeremiah 49 talks of troops falling and being silenced in the streets.

In other words, as I take up writing this booklet once again in July 2013, we see various wars, rebellions, geopolitical posturing and events taking place immediately around Israel that will put all the actors of the Psalm 83 confederation into place. And when the war eventually starts, as surely it must, it will be a war with a united and determined and very, very strong Israel fighting superior numbers of enemy under God's guidance. The victory against Hezbolllah, Hamas, Fatah, Syria, Lebanon, troops from Iraq, Jordan and the Gaza strip (or radicals living in those countries) will be so total that these forces will be decimated forever, leading to a period of PEACE the likes of which Israel has never experienced. But more about that in coming chapters.

'Simplified summary'

When you see Israel go to war with Hezbollah, Hamas, Fatah, Al Qaida and Salafists in its immediate neighbours, you will know the Psalm 83 war has commenced. This will happen after Israel has tolerated *extreme provocation*.

b) The Ezekiel 38 war

The scriptures in Ezekiel 38 indicate that Israel will be living in un-walled villages when it is attacked from the north. This is a very profound statement considering Israel has never lived in un-walled villages in all of its history and even more so since Israel became a nation in 1948.

So, how could this be achieved? Well, we have just read in earlier chapters that Israel goes to war with its neighbours and thoroughly defeats them to the point that they never rise again to fight her. If the Psalm 83 scenario is true then, this massive defeat of all radical forces surrounding Israel will result in a period of peace not known or experienced before, for the people of Israel. I believe that Israel will let her guard down and may very well start erecting villages without walls or even tear down the huge wall that divides parts of the country now.

I believe it will be a period of peace and prosperity like never before. The prosperity will come from the wealth of the Tamar and Levathian gas fields Israel owns, which is one of the largest in the world and where there is gas there is oil.

I have been interested in end times events for the last quarter of a century and as long as twenty five years ago I said to my best friend Pat that when Israel hits gas or oil it will result in the invasion if Israel. I have waited two and a half decades for this possibility to become reality. (Author: Oct 2015 – Israel has hit a massive oil reserve in the Golan heights!!! In disputed territory, it couldn't get better than that to start a war)

I postulate that as soon as the dust of the Psalm 83 war settles and the dead are buried, that peace will cover the land and Israel will start trading its oil and gas and build up its magnificent agricultural system to the very best and possibly the biggest in the world. It will export breath-taking new technologies and grow in wealth and prestige for several years.

But remember, there will be anger, jealousy and resentment in the Muslim world and particularly the patrons of the former forces crushed by Israel. To them, it will be a time of gathering strength for pay-back. It will be a time to build forces for the elimination of Israel once and for all.

The trigger for this 'pay-back' against Israel will, I believe, be the demise of the Russian natural gas system that supplies Europe with most of its domestic heating and cooking needs.

As Russian gas supplies reduce, or even if they don't, the huge, glittering prize of Israel's gas and oil fields will be a severe temptation to attack Israel, especially if the USA is involved in a civil war or has gone to war with China over South Korea or more likely, that Europe starts buying Israeli liquid gas over Russia's. In any event, Russia will attack Israel for both pay-back (as she is the patron supplier and economic partner of many Muslim nations) and economic reasons. At least that is how secular people will view this invasion. But behind the scenes, the reason will be spiritual as is clearly laid out in Ezekiel 38 when Gog is called forth to attack Israel.

The purpose of this booklet is not to go into too much detail but the reader can study Gog for him/herself. It is quite clear from scripture that Gog is mentioned in the old testament at least twice and once in Revelation 20. In view of the fact that Gog's lifespan covers millennia, it's safe to assume Gog is a name for an evil spirit or 'strongman'. He is probably the equivalent of Michael or Gabriel in seniority and would dominate or rule over the dark spiritual forces that cover Russia. It is *he* a powerful demonic spirit, that persuades the human leaders of Russia to join forces with many other nations to attack Israel and smash her once and for all.

It is pure conjecture but I think the human leader that Gog will persuade to attack Israel is Putin himself. I believe we are that close to these events happening and it is clear to see that Putin is setting himself up to be President of Russia indefinitely, with his constant arrests and harassment of the opposition. But, let's turn back to the Bible and see what it says, as that is where all truth rests. We will read Ezekiel 38/39 now.

Ezekiel 38/39 *(Italics by the author)*

38 Now the word of the Lord came to me, saying, ² 'Son of man, set your face against Gog, *[Gog is a strong demon in the same order as Michael and is mentioned in the Greek Septuagint, in Amos 7:1-2, Ezekiel 38 and Revelation 20]* of the land of Magog *[Soviet union]*, the prince of Rosh *[Russia]*, Meshech *[Balkans]*, and Tubal *[Turkey]*, and prophesy against him, ³ and say, 'Thus says the Lord God: Behold, I *am* against you, O Gog, the prince of Rosh, Meshech, and Tubal *[Parts of former soviet union?]*. ⁴ I will turn you around, put hooks into your jaws, and lead you out, with all your army, horses, and horsemen, all splendidly clothed, a great company *with* bucklers and shields, all of them handling swords. ⁵ Persia, *[Iran]* Ethiopia,[b] and Libya[c] are with them, all of them *with* shield and helmet; ⁶ Gomer *[Countries north of Balkans]* and all its troops; the house of Togarmah *[Georgia through Turkmenistan, Uzbekistan and Kazakhstan] from* the far north and all its troops—many people *are* with you.

⁷ 'Prepare yourself and be ready, you and all your companies that are gathered about you; and be a guard for them. ⁸ After many days you will be visited. In the latter years you will come into the land of those brought back from the sword *and* gathered from many people on the mountains of Israel, which had long been desolate; they were brought out of the nations, *and now all of them dwell safely.* ⁹ You will ascend, coming like a storm, covering the land like a cloud, you and all your troops and many peoples with you.'

¹⁰ 'Thus says the Lord God: 'On that day it shall come to pass *that* thoughts

will arise in your mind, and you will make an evil plan: ¹¹ You will say, 'I will go up *against a land of un-walled villages;* I will go to a peaceful people, who dwell safely, all of them dwelling without walls, and having neither bars nor gates'— ¹² to take plunder and to take booty, to stretch out your hand against the waste places *that are again* inhabited, and against a people gathered from the nations, who have acquired livestock and goods, who dwell in the midst of the land. ¹³ Sheba, Dedan *(Saudi Arabia),* the merchants of Tarshish, and all their young lions *(basically all western nations)* will say to you, 'Have you come to take plunder? Have you gathered your army to take booty, to carry away silver and gold, to take away livestock and goods, to take great plunder?'"

¹⁴ 'Therefore, son of man, prophesy and say to Gog, 'Thus says the Lord God: 'On that day when My people Israel dwell safely, will you not know *it?* ¹⁵ Then you will come from your place out of the far north, you and many peoples with you, all of them riding on horses, a great company and a mighty army. ¹⁶ You will come up against My people Israel like a cloud, to cover the land. It will be in the latter days that I will bring you against My land, so that the nations may know Me, when I am hallowed in you, O Gog, before their eyes.' ¹⁷ Thus says the Lord God: 'Are *you* he of whom I have spoken in former days by My servants the prophets of Israel, who prophesied for years in those days that I would bring you against them?

Judgment on Gog

¹⁸ 'And it will come to pass at the same time, when Gog comes against the land of Israel,' says the Lord God, '*that* My fury will show in My face. ¹⁹ For in My jealousy *and* in the fire of My wrath I have spoken: 'Surely in that day there shall be a great earthquake in the land of Israel, ²⁰ so that the fish of the sea, the birds of the Heavens, the beasts of the field, all creeping things that creep on the Earth, and all men who *are* on the face of the Earth shall shake at My presence. The mountains shall be thrown down, the steep places shall fall, and every wall shall fall to the ground.' ²¹ I will call for a sword against Gog throughout all My mountains,' says the Lord God. 'Every man's sword will be against his brother. ²² *[Sunni/Shia split?]* And I will bring him to judgment with pestilence and bloodshed; I will rain down on him, on his troops, and on the many peoples who *are* with him, flooding rain, great hailstones, fire, and brimstone. ²³ Thus I will magnify Myself and sanctify Myself, and I will be known in the eyes of many nations. Then they shall know that I *am* the Lord.'

Here are a few things we can deduce from these scriptures:

- Israel is attacked when it is at peace in un-walled villages.
- The nations mentioned in the Psalm 83 war are not mentioned in this event, giving evidence to the theory that the Psalm 83 war precedes Ezekiel 38/39.
- The Psalm 83 war and the Ezekiel 38/39 event will destroy all of Islam's armies in the middle-east but not Islam itself nor its populations, who will recover quickly under the Antichrist.
- The victory will be a supernatural event that is not assisted by the Israeli military.
- People all over the world, including Israel, will recognize God's hand in this victory and turn to Him in their millions.

Further notes on Ezekiel 38 and the Gog/Magog 'wars'.

There is one thread in end-time events that causes great confusion in people's minds and confounds or confuses their ability to fit certain prophetic events into a sensible timeline.

The main area of confusion is whether Ezekiel 38's invasion of Israel, which clearly talks about Gog and Magog, is the one and the same event as the Gog/Magog 'war' in Revelation 20. Linking these two scenarios makes many people believe, in error, that there is no Invasion of Israel until the end of the Millennium, the thousand year period of peace that immediately follows Christ's second coming, and this belief completely destroys an obvious and very pending timeline event, the soon invasion of Israel by Russia and her allies.

It must be noted that the Gog/Magog events are not wars, as it is God Himself that destroys the armies gathered against Israel, although some commentators acknowledge that the ancient language used to describe these prophecies could be terminology for nuclear war. Whatever the case, both Gog/Magog events end in the destruction of Israel's enemies. And they are clearly destroyed in different ways.

In the Ezekiel 38 scenario, the enemies are defeated by a world-wide earthquake, rain, pestilence, hailstones and brimstone (a phrase commonly confused for nuclear war, hence the confusion) while the scenario depicted in Revelation 20 ends through fire from Heaven. This clearly indicates these are two totally separate events and must not confuse the student of eschatology (end time study) as to when they will happen, thus throwing out the timeline of coming events. It's rather like WW1 being followed some time later by WW2. Finally, the Ezekiel event lists specific nations that attack Israel while Revelation 20 speaks of the entire world coming against Israel.

'Simplified Summary'

When you see Iran join forces with Turkey (whom it hates as one is Shia and the other is Sunni) and comes under the leadership of Russia and other states around the black sea, you will know the Ezekiel 38 'war' is about to kick off. As I edit this in 2018 this very thing has happened, the three principal nations, Russia, Turkey and Iran are now allies.

Let's continue with the remaining three scriptures that help explain the 'when' of all these events

c) Isaiah 66: 6-8

This scripture predicts that the nation of Israel will be reborn in *one day* as it did on May 14th 1948. Another scripture prophesies this to the exact day from the 2nd Temple period in the 5th century BC and that is Ezekiel 4: 3-6. This is key to anchoring when the Rapture, the Psalm 83 war and Ezekiel 38 will take place, as it is the generation that sees Israel become a nation that will see the end times *commence.*

d) Matthew 24:34

This scripture states that people born in 1948 will see the end times events start 70 years hence (2018). Although a generation is referred to I think it's safe to say a life span is what is meant, as God has actually told us we live 'three score and ten years' (70 years). A generational period brings forth argument as some people say it's 40 years and others say it's 50 years based on the Jewish Jubilee cycle. I will choose the former for the purposes of this book.

e) Daniel's 70 weeks prophecy

Daniel's prophecies are so incredibly accurate, and as time passes, easier to understand, that many critics have claimed that the prophecies were written *after* our Lord died on the cross. This is absurd of course because the Greeks translated it into the Septuagint over 300 years before Christ was born. It is this book, along with other major prophetic books in the Bible, that give us two basic tenets upon which we can fashion our end time philosophy. The first is that the last seven years of human history before the millennium, is for God to turn His attention back to dealing with the Jews, rather than the Church or the unbelieving gentile. It is this fact that readily supports the pre-tribulation Rapture because God's main focus will be on the restoration of Israel.

Secondly, vivid descriptions of the Antichrist and exciting titbits of information start to collate into who, where and whence the Antichrist originates and it is these prophecies that once again support the pre-tribulation Rapture theory. For the reader that does not understand the importance of Daniel's seventy weeks prophecy, here is a simple overview.

❧ ☙

(The following material is taken from Jack Kelley's superb website GraceThrufaith.com, with his kind permission)

'Daniel was an old man, probably in his eighties. He'd been in Babylon for nearly 70 years and knew from reading the recently completed scroll of Jeremiah's writings (specifically the part we know as **Jeremiah 25:8-11**) that the 70-year captivity God had ordained for Israel was just about over (**Daniel 9:2**).

The reason for the captivity had been Israel's insistence upon worshiping the false gods of their pagan neighbours. Its duration of 70 years came from the fact that for 490 years they had failed to let their farmland lie fallow one year out of every seven as God had commanded in **Leviticus 25:1-7**. The Lord had been patient all that time but finally had sent them to Babylon to give the land the 70 years of rest that were due it. (**2 Chronicles 36:21**)

The beginning of **Daniel 9** documents Daniel's prayer, reminding the Lord that the 70 year time of punishment was nearly over and asking for mercy on behalf of his people. Before he could finish his prayer, the angel Gabriel appeared to him and spoke the words that we know as **Daniel 9:24-27**. Let's read the whole thing to get the overview and then take it apart verse by verse.

Seventy weeks are determined upon your people and your Holy City to finish transgression, to put an end to sin, to atone for wickedness, to bring in everlasting righteousness, to seal up vision and prophecy and to anoint the most Holy. Know and understand this: From the issuing of the decree to restore and rebuild Jerusalem until The Anointed One the Ruler comes there will be seven weeks and sixty two weeks. It will be rebuilt with streets and a trench but in times of trouble. After the sixty two weeks the Anointed One will be cut off and have nothing. The people of the ruler who will come will destroy the city and the sanctuary. The end will come like a flood: War will continue till the end and desolations have been decreed. He will confirm a covenant with many for one week. In the middle of the week he will put an end to sacrifice and offering. And on a wing of the Temple he will set up an abomination that causes desolation until the end that is decreed is poured out on him (**Daniel 9:24-27**).

No prophecy in all of Scripture is more critical to our understanding of the end times than these four verses. A few basic clarifications are in order first, then we'll interpret the passage verse by verse. The Hebrew word translated weeks (or sevens) refers to a period of 7 years, like the English word decade refers to a period of 10 years. It literally means 'a week of years.' So 70 weeks is 70 x 7 years or 490 years. This period is divided into three parts, 7 weeks or 49 years, 62 weeks or 434 years, and 1 week or 7 years. Let's begin.

Seventy weeks are determined upon your people and your Holy City to finish transgression, to put an end to sin, to atone for wickedness, to bring in everlasting righteousness, to seal up vision and prophecy and to anoint the most Holy (place) (**Daniel 9:24**).

Sitting upon His Heavenly throne, God decreed that six things would be accomplished for Daniel's people (Israel) and Daniel's Holy City (Jerusalem) during a specified period of 490 years. (I've inserted the word 'place' after Holy at the end of the verse to clarify the fact that it refers to the Jewish Temple in Jerusalem.)

We should be aware that in Hebrew these things read a little differently. Literally, God had determined to;

1. restrict or restrain <u>the</u> transgression (also translated rebellion)
2. seal up their sins (as if putting them away in a sealed container)
3. make atonement (restitution) for their iniquity
4. bring them into a state of everlasting righteousness
5. seal up (same word as #2) vision and prophecy
6. anoint (consecrate) the most Holy place (sanctuary)

In plain language, God would put an end to their rebellion against Him, put away their sins and pay the penalties they had accrued, bring the people into a state of perpetual righteousness, fulfil the remaining prophecies, and anoint the Temple. This was to be accomplished through their Messiah (Jesus) because no one else could do it. Had they accepted Him as their saviour their rebellion against God would have ended. Their sins would have all been forgiven, and the full penalty paid for them. They would have entered into a state of eternal righteousness, all their prophecies would have been fulfilled and the rebuilt temple would have been consecrated. It should be noted here that although it appears to have been accepted by Him, God never dwelt in the 2nd Temple, nor was the ark of the covenant and its mercy seat ever present therein.

Know and understand this: From the issuing of the decree to restore and rebuild Jerusalem until The Anointed One the Ruler comes there will be seven weeks and sixty two weeks. It will be rebuilt with streets and a trench but in times of trouble (**Daniel 9:25**).

Here is a clear prophecy of the timing of the First Coming. When this message was given to Daniel by the angel Gabriel, Jerusalem had lain in ruin for nearly 70 years and the Jews were captive in Babylon. Counting forward for 62 + 7 periods of 7 years each (a total of 483 years) from a future decree giving the Jews permission to restore and rebuild Jerusalem, they should expect the Messiah.

To avoid confusion, it's important to distinguish the decree that freed the Jews from their captivity from the one that gave them permission to rebuild Jerusalem.

When he conquered Babylon in 535BC Cyrus the Persian immediately freed the Jews. It had been prophesied 150 years earlier in **Isaiah 44:24-45:6** and was fulfilled in **Ezra 1:1-4**. But according to **Nehemiah 2:1-9** the decree to rebuild Jerusalem was given in the first month of the 20th year of his reign by King Artaxerxes of Persia (March of 445 BC on our calendar, about 90 years later).

About 125 years ago Sir Robert Anderson unlocked the secret of Daniel's 70 weeks when he teamed up with the London Royal Observatory to discover that prophetic years are 360 days in length and consist of 12 months of 30 days each. This is also the only way you can make the three measures of the Great Tribulation (1260 days, 42 months, or 3 1/2 years) come out the same. Therefore the 70 weeks of Daniel consist of 490 years of 360 days each. He published this discovery in a book called The Coming Prince, a commentary on Daniel's 70th Week.

From their research we also know that exactly 483 years after the decree of Artaxerxes the Lord Jesus rode in to Jerusalem on a donkey to shouts of 'Hosanna'! It was the only day in His life that He permitted His followers to proclaim Him as Israel's King, fulfilling Daniel's prophecy to the day! The Hebrew in **Daniel 9:25** calls Him Messiah the Prince, denoting the fact that He was coming as the Anointed Son of the King and was not yet crowned King Himself.

THE FUTURE MONTHS AND YEARS TO THE END

In **Luke 19:41-45**, Jesus reminded the people of the specific nature of this prophecy. As he approached Jerusalem and saw the city, he wept over it and said, *'If you, even you, had only known on this day what would bring you peace–but now it is hidden from your eyes. The days will come upon you when your enemies will build an embankment against you and encircle you and hem you in on every side. They will dash you to the ground, you and the children within your walls. They will not leave one stone on another, because you did not recognize the time of God's coming to you.'* He held them accountable for knowing **Daniel 9:24-27**.

A few days later He extended that accountability to those who would be alive in Israel during the End Times. *'So when you see standing in the holy place 'the abomination that causes desolation,' spoken of through the prophet Daniel– let the reader understand– then let those who are in Judea flee to the mountains.* (**Matthew 24:15-16**) They will also be required to understand **Daniel 9**.

After the sixty two weeks the Anointed One will be cut off and have nothing. The people of the ruler who will come will destroy the city and the sanctuary. The end will come like a flood: War will continue till the end and desolations have been decreed (**Daniel 9:26**).

First came 7 sevens (49 years) and then 62 sevens (434 years) for a total of 69 sevens or 483 years. The Hebrew word for Anointed One is Mashaich (Messiah in English). At the end of this 2nd period their Messiah would be cut off, which means to be executed or literally destroyed in the making of a covenant, having received none of the honour, glory and blessing the Scriptures promised Him.

Make no mistake about it. Jesus had to die so these 6 promises could come true. No one else in Heaven or on Earth could accomplish this. We can only imagine how different things would have been if they had accepted Him as their Messiah and let Him die for their sins so He could bring them into everlasting righteousness with His resurrection. But of course God knew they wouldn't, so He had to do things the hard way.

Do you realize what that means? It wasn't killing the Messiah that put the Jews at odds with God. After all He came to die for them. No. It's that in killing Him, they refused to let His death pay for their sins so He could save them. This had the effect of making His death meaningless to them. That's what severed the relationship. Because of that, we now get the first hint that all would not go well. Following the crucifixion the people of a ruler yet to come would destroy Jerusalem and the Temple, the same Temple that God decreed would be consecrated. The Israelites would be scattered abroad and peace would elude the world.

We all know that Jesus was crucified and 38 years later the Romans put the torch to the city and the Temple destroying both. Surviving Jews were forced to flee for their lives and in the ensuing 2000 years I don't believe a single generation has escaped involvement in a war of some kind.

After the crucifixion something strange happened: The Heavenly clock stopped. 69 of the 70 weeks had passed and all that was prophesied to happen during those 483 years had come to pass but there was still one week (7 years) left. There are hints in the Old Testament that the clock had stopped several times before in Israel's history when for one reason or another they were either under subjugation or out of the land. And in the New Testament we're also given hints that while God is dealing with the Church, time ceases to exist for Israel (**Acts 15:13-18**). But the clearest indication of the stopped clock is that the events foretold in **Daniel 9:27** simply haven't happened yet.

He will confirm a covenant with many for one week. In the middle of the week he will put an end to sacrifice and offering. And on a wing of the Temple he will set up an abomination that causes desolation until the end that is decreed is poured out on him(**9:27**).

It's vital to our understanding of the End Times that we realize two things here. First, the Age of Grace didn't follow the Age of Law, it merely interrupted the Age of Law seven years short of its promised duration. These seven years have to be completed for God to accomplish the six things the angel listed in verse 24 for Israel.

And second, the Age of Grace was not the next step in the progression of God's overall plan, but was a deviation from it. Once the Rapture comes, nothing like the Age of Grace will ever happen again (**Ephesians 2:6-7**). Even when Israel accepts the New Covenant, as **Jeremiah 31:31-34** promises, they won't enjoy the same benefits the Church has enjoyed. The relationship the Church has with the Lord will never be repeated with any other group. Ever.

But before we try to understand the 70th week let's review a rule of grammar that will help make our interpretation of verse 27 correct. The rule is this: Pronouns refer us back to the closest previous noun. 'He', being a personal pronoun, refers to the closest previous personal noun, in this case 'the ruler who will come.' So a ruler who will come from the territory of the old Roman Empire will confirm a 7 year covenant with Israel that permits them to build a Temple and re-instate their Old Covenant worship system.

3 1/2 years later he will violate the covenant by setting up an abomination that causes the Temple to become desolate, putting an end to their worship. This abomination brings the wrath of God down upon him and he will be destroyed.

The most obvious way in which we know these things haven't happened is that the Jewish Old Covenant worship system requires a Temple and there hasn't been one since 70 AD when the Romans destroyed it.

Some say this prophecy was fulfilled during the Roman destruction but most believe it's yet future, partly because of the term Abomination that causes Desolation. It's a specific insult to God that has happened only once previously. Antiochus Epiphanes, a powerful Syrian king, had attacked Jerusalem and entered the Temple area in 168BC. There he had sacrificed a pig on the Temple altar and erected a statue of the Greek god Zeus with his own face on it. He then required everyone to worship it on pain of death. This rendered the Temple unfit for worshiping God and so incensed the Jews that they revolted and defeated the Syrians. This is all recorded in Jewish history (1st Maccabees) where it's called the Abomination of Desolation. The subsequent cleansing of the Temple is celebrated to this day in the Feast of Hanukkah.

Paul warned us that in the latter days a world leader will become so powerful that he will exalt himself above everything that is called god or is worshiped and will stand in the Temple proclaiming himself to be God (**2 Thessalonians 2:4**). In **Revelation 13:14-15** we're told that he'll have a statue of himself erected and require everyone to worship it on pain of death. In **Matthew 24:15-21** Jesus said that the Abomination that causes Desolation spoken of by Daniel will kick off the Great Tribulation, a period of time 3 1/2 years long that coincides with the last half of Daniel's 70th week. The similarities between this coming event and the one from history being so obvious, most scholars are persuaded that one points to the other since nothing in the intervening years fits so completely.

Soon And Very Soon
A new leader will soon emerge on the scene, a man with great personal charisma. Following a devastating war in the Middle East he'll present a plan to restore peace, by which he will quickly captivate and control the world. Since all true believers will have recently disappeared from Earth in the Rapture of the Church, he'll have no trouble persuading most remaining

inhabitants that he is the promised Messiah, the Prince of Peace. He will astound and amaze them all with feats of diplomacy and conquest, even performing the supernatural.

When he claims to be God, all hell will break loose on Earth and 3 1/2 years of the most terrible times mankind has ever known will threaten their very existence. But before they're all destroyed the real Prince of Peace will return and overthrow this impostor. He will set up His kingdom on Earth, a kingdom that will never be destroyed or left to another.

Having given His life to finish transgression, put an end to sin, atone for wickedness and bring in everlasting righteousness, and having fulfilled all Biblical vision and prophecy, He will anoint the most Holy Place and receive all the honour, glory and blessing the Scriptures promise Him. Israel will finally have her Kingdom back and will live in peace with God in her midst forever.']

⚬ ⚬

'Simplified Summary'

God's disciplining of the Jews was put on hold when Christ went to the cross, leaving seven years of their disciplining to a future time, at the conclusion of which total restoration of the Jewish people (those who are left alive by that stage) will occur; a seven year period seeing the Church in Heaven, attending the Bema seat 'judgement' and the wedding, among many other wonders while on Earth many millions of new Christians struggle to stay alive under a brutal world-wide regime controlled by the Antichrist.

We have just read five scriptures, when taken together in context, fix the timing of the Rapture, the Tribulation and the Second Coming of Christ. In a nutshell the events described in Psalm 83 and Ezekiel 38 should start to come to fruition within 70 years of Israel being reborn in 1948. The first sign will be the Psalm 83 war (which is imminent in 2018), then the Rapture and the Ezekiel 38 war happening almost simultaneously, (a few years after the Psalm 83 war) followed by the confirmation of the peace treaty with Israel by the Antichrist and then seven years of Tribulation, at the end of which Jesus returns to crush and remove all evil people from Earth.

Chapter 4

The Rapture

To put it simply, when the Church, The Bride of Christ, has taken in its last brother or sister into its ranks, decided by God Himself, the Church will leave planet Earth and be 'caught up' into the air to meet with Jesus, the 'bridegroom', where He will escort us in our new, immortal bodies, to Heaven. The arrival of Christ in our atmosphere must not be confused with Christ's Second Coming, that happens at the end of the Great Tribulation, when He returns to crush evil and set up His one thousand year Kingdom on Earth.

The Rapture will happen when the full number of gentiles is in the Church (Romans 11:25) and we are told it will happen before the Tribulation in Romans 5: 9 ; 1 Corinthians 15: 51-53; 1 Thessalonians 1:10; 1 Thessalonians 5: 9; 1 Thessalonians 4: 16-17 and Revelation 3:10 . The word Rapture is not used but the Greek word Harpazo was translated into the word Rapture in Latin and is labelled as being 'caught up' in English. 1 Thessalonians 4: 17 is the scripture to refer to.

There are three views on the Rapture:

- The Church is Raptured (taken away) from Earth before the end times Tribulation commences.
- The Church is Raptured halfway through the Tribulation.
- The Church is Raptured at the end of the Tribulation and immediately returns with Christ to Earth.

For the purposes of this book I am choosing the pre-tribulation scenario as it fits Daniel's 70th week prophecy and Revelation far more closely than mid or post Tribulation scenarios. There is also much supporting evidence to this viewpoint but before we look at the evidence, let's look at four main examples of what many people use as an argument against a pre-Tribulation Rapture. One of the main arguments is that the Antichrist wars with the saints during the Great Tribulation and that millions die at his hand. This has persuaded many Christians, particularly in the USA, to buy huge amounts of ammunition and food to fend off the coming system of Antichrist that will enter the world.

THE END TIMES SIMPLIFIED

Secondly, another common argument is that no Christian is exempt from the evils of the world, with massacres from the Roman days to murder in modern-day Nigeria, Egypt and Syria as prime examples. Thirdly, some believers think we will suffer the first three and a half years and then suddenly get yanked off the Earth as the Great Tribulation starts while others feel we will go through the whole Tribulation up to the second coming. Both Philosophies rest on the premise that we somehow need to be 'refined' before lifting off the Earth, as if Christ's dreadful death on the cross was not sufficient for us, nor God the Father. Fourthly, the Tribulation is called Satan's wrath by many and not God's wrath, thus conveniently neutralising 1 Thessalonians 5:9 which states that the church will not face God's *wrath*.

To counter these arguments we to need study the literal interpretation of the Bible (exegesis) and accept that in many cases, especially in the book of Revelation, that the Bible is written chronologically, with some chapters being a summary or continuation of prior thoughts John was putting down on paper. If the reader does some deep study you will find that the seal, trumpet and bowl judgements follow each other chronologically, with the seal judgements not only coinciding with the beginning of the Tribulation but also coinciding with the very start of Daniel's 70th week prophecy.

To counter the four main reasons why people do not accept a pre-Tribulation Rapture, let's consider the following:

- Saints may indeed be killed by the Antichrist system but these saints will *not* be the Church. The saints that are warred against during the Tribulation are those that turn to Christ in their millions after the Rapture and the war of Ezekiel 38/39. As I stated earlier, the destruction of the Islamic armies by supernatural events that exclude the destruction of Israel, will make many millions of people realise that God's promises supporting Israel's eternal existence is real and that therefore God must after all exist. The Fascist-Marxist/Islamic New World Order that the Antichrist will control will soon turn on these new believers and massacre them in untold numbers. These are the believers that cry out to God from under the altar in Revelation 6. In Revelation 5, the elders are praising another group of believers that are *already* in Heaven, calling them Kings! You will notice that if Revelation is chronological, then as surely as chapter 5 precedes chapter 6, so does the arrival in Heaven of another group of Christians called the Church (Kings) precede the arrival of the martyred saints.
- The murder of Christians over the ages has never been considered from the

wrath of God. God's wrath (in the end-times context) is restricted to the last seven years of human history before the millennium. People who enter this time-slot are *not* the Church that is spoken of in 1Thessalonians 5:9, because people that enter the Tribulation are unsaved, only turning to Christ *after* the Rapture. Yes, Christians will face persecution but *not* Wrath; this is very important to understand.

- The idea that we have to be refined by a dreadful seven year period on Earth to somehow 'qualify' us to be Raptured or enter Heaven is a complete insult to what Christ did for us on the cross. It is complete anathema to me, the author, that after Christ suffered so dreadfully prior to and on the cross, that we still have to work out some type of cleansing process to be counted 'worthy'. One only has to watch Mel Gibson's very realistic '*The Passion*' to see the absolute horror that Christ endured for our sins to be assured of the fact that there is absolutely nothing more we can do to enter Heaven other than believe in Jesus. *Nothing*! Besides, why would this particular group of believers be the only lot in the whole of human history that has to face refinement through wrath? Persecution, which Christians have endured for so long, is not wrath from God.

- Many scholars have called the Great Tribulation 'Satan's wrath'. Their error comes from Revelation 12:12 where Satan is described as being really angry and full of wrath. However, he is angry at being removed from Heaven! He is the *subject* of God's wrath, not the *author* of it! The whole seven year Tribulation is God's wrath.

That answers the four main claims against a pre-Tribulation Rapture, but here are some more comments that support the pre-Tribulation scenario.

- The Great Tribulation is properly interpreted by pre-Tribulationists as a time of preparation for Israel's restoration (Deuteronomy. 4:29-30; Jeremiah. 30: 4-11). It is not the purpose of the Tribulation to prepare the church for glory.

- Pre-Tribulationism maintains the scriptural distinction between the Great Tribulation and tribulation in general that precedes it.

- None of the Old Testament passages on the Tribulation mention the church (Deuteronomy 4: 29-30; Jeremiah 30: 4-11; Daniel. 8:24-27; 12:1-2).

- The unity of Daniel's seventieth week is maintained by pre-Tribulationists. By contrast, post-Tribulationism and mid-Tribulationists destroy the unity of Daniel's seventieth week *and confuse Israel's programme with that of the church.*

- The translation of the Church is never mentioned in any passage dealing with the second coming of Christ, after the Tribulation.

- The Church is not appointed to God's wrath (Romans. 5:9: 1 Thessalonians. 1:9-10; 5:9). The Church therefore cannot enter "the great day of their wrath" (Revelation 6:17).
- The Church will not be overtaken by the 'Day of the Lord' (1 Thessalonians 5:1-9), which includes the Tribulation.
- The possibility of a believer escaping the Tribulation is mentioned in Luke 21:36.
- The church of Philadelphia was promised deliverance from "the hour of trial that is going to come upon the whole world to test those who live on the Earth" (Revelation 3:10).
- It is characteristic of divine dealing to deliver believers before a divine judgment is inflicted on the world, as illustrated in the deliverance of Noah, Lot, Rahab, etc. (2 Peter 2:5-9). Persecution of believers in the past must not be confused with God's wrath. Wrath and persecution are different.
- At the time of the translation of the Church, all believers go to the Father's house in Heaven (John 14:3) and do not immediately return to the Earth after meeting Christ in the air as post-Tribulationists teach. Post-Tribulation allows no time for the Bema-seat judgment to take place!
- The pre-Tribulational interpretation teaches that the coming of Christ is actually imminent. The exhortation to look for "the glorious appearing" of Christ to His own (Titus 2:13) loses its significance if the Tribulation must intervene first.
- The Holy Spirit, as the restrainer of evil, cannot have His influence removed from the world unless the Church, which the Spirit indwells, is translated at the same time. The Tribulation cannot begin until this restraint is lifted. I believe the 'restrainer' is the Holy Spirit and not an angel as some people surmise (2 Thessalonians 2 :7).
- A pre-Tribulation Rapture will accelerate the demise of the USA (as the USA has many Christians) before Russia attacks Israel as described in Ezekiel 39/39. America's demise will give Russia the boldness it needs to attack Israel.

In concluding this section on the Rapture, I would like to postulate that the following time-line will occur:

- The Psalm 83 war takes place.
- Peace and security (not the *false* peace ad safety of the Antichrist) follows for a

short while.

- The Rapture occurs 'out of the blue'. (Many scriptures support it's sudden, very unexpected happening). America, with its very large Christian population will be greatly weakened as a nation, whereas Russia [which now has 40% Muslim soldiers], Europe [50 million Muslims], China [few believers], India [Hindu] and all the Arabic nations [Islamic] will hardly notice the Rapture at all, at a local level of course, but corporately will result in hundreds of millions of people coming to Christ.

- The '*war*' described in Ezekiel 38/39 will occur. I put the word 'war' in Italics because God Himself kills off Israel's enemies through natural events.

- Daniel's 70th week commences as does the Tribulation itself. They are one and the same. This is when God deals with Israel's final seven years of punishment., although many Jews will accept Christ and be supernaturally protected by Michael the Arch Angel in Petra. The early part of the Tribulation will see the rapid rise of a very powerful and influential man that will later become known as the Antichrist, three and a half years into Daniel's 70th week.

Chapter 5

The Antichrist

The coming Antichrist is a hot topic for many Christians, for, once again, Christians are divided on the subject. Some Christians believe the Antichrist has come and gone, while others believe the destruction of Jerusalem in AD 70 and a second rebellion by the Jews against the Romans in the second century AD fulfilled all of Daniel's prophecies. This is called Preterism and must be avoided like the plague. Yet others believe the age of the Jew is over and that somehow we as Christians have replaced the Jews as God's chosen people. Neither approach is correct.

For this study on the Antichrist, I turn once again to the books of Daniel and Revelation as they are perhaps the most accurate books when it comes to determining the *who, when, where* of this soon-to-come, infamous world leader. It is a complicated subject so I will try and keep it simple.

The best place to start is the statue of Nebuchadnezzar, the King of Babylon during the period the Jews were held captive there, for the 70 year period mentioned earlier.

The king had an odd dream in which he saw a huge statue made up of different metals. None of his wise men could interpret the dream but eventually Daniel was remembered as being a man that could interpret dreams and was brought before the king. After some consideration Daniel interpreted the dream. He told the king that the statue represented four kingdoms. The head, made of Gold, represented Nebuchadnezzar's Kingdom, while the chest of silver represented the coming Medo-Persian Kingdom, followed by the Greek Empire, represented by a Bronze skirt, followed a final Roman Empire, represented by Iron. Part of the dream showed a stone about to dash the feet of the statue. More on this later though.

Daniel's interpretation of the dream regarded various kingdoms to follow, as an inanimate statue (Daniel 2: 36-44), while God's view of the future (from the same point in time) was interpreted through various animals (Daniel 8:20). Daniel 2 is therefore *confirmed* in Daniel 8 and is not a separate event.

God saw the Babylonian Kingdom as a Lion with wings. It is interesting to note that when Saddam Hussein started to rebuild Babylon, he built a huge temple with two of these very statues at the front gate. Medo-Persia was seen by God as a bear (this was the very kingdom that would free the Jews from captivity) while the Greek Empire is shown as a Leopard. Alexander the Great's empire grew so rapidly that it covered the ground like a Leopard, which is possibly one reason why God chose this symbol for that empire. And finally, God saw the Roman Empire as a terrible beast. The legs represent Rome up to its dissolution in the middle ages while the feet and toes represent a resurrected Roman Empire.

This exciting revelation of what is to come, right down to the end of ages, is mirrored in *reverse order* in the book of Revelation but before I come on to that, what is the stone that is about to strike the feet of the resurrected Roman empire? It is none other than a rock cut without (human) hands, thus describing the returning Christ and His Kingdom, dashing to pieces the final, resurrected Roman Empire at the end of the Great Tribulation.

John's vision of the future, in Revelation, is in reverse order to Daniel's viewpoint of the future for the simple reason that the Bible is written chronologically. Daniel lived many hundreds of years before John did. Daniel lived in the Babylonian era whereas John lived in the Roman era. Therefore, John's vision looks both backwards and forwards as described in Revelation 13: 1-2 and 17: 9-11, while Daniel's interpretation only looks *forward*.

John saw *five* empires before him, namely Egypt, Assyria, Babylon, Persia and Greece. He was alive in the 6th Empire's reign (Rome) and foresaw a 7th Empire, the revived Roman Empire.

But John's vision goes on to state that out of the 7th Empire, which has ten horns (Kings) in it, an 8th King will arise, not only as the 8th King in the long line of empires, but also as the eleventh King of the ten Kings (horns) that belong to the 7th Empire. The 8th King and the 11th King are therefore one and the same (*from Daniel's viewpoint*).

It is this King, which *comes from the 5th Empire in Daniel's timeline, including his own Kingdom* (and is the same king as John's 8th King) that is the Antichrist and we must turn our attention to him in order to understand who the Antichrist is and possibly where he comes from.

It is the 5th empire in Daniel's interpretation of Nebuchanedzzar's dream and the 7th empire of John's vision that indicates the Antichrist comes from the *revived* Roman empire and is of Roman lineage; indeed the very people that destroyed Jerusalem in AD70. Daniel 9:26-27 confirms this quite clearly.

For centuries Christians looked for this revived Roman empire as a sign of the end of times, so it's understandable that when the European Union was first formed in 1993 there was great excitement in the Christian world that the 5th/7th Empire was being resurrected, as it was formed under the Rome treaty of 1958 and covered the very countries that were included in the Roman empire of AD70. This led to numerous speculation that one of the Popes would become the Antichrist and that the Roman Catholic Church would be the spiritual harlot.

My view, however, is totally different, for while scripture says the Antichrist comes from the Roman empire, it does not say which *part* of the empire, the original western empire headquartered in Rome or the eastern empire headquartered (originally) in what is modern day Split and subsequently in Constantinople. The choice of which part of the Roman Empire the Antichrist comes from bears huge consequences for your interpretation of where the Antichrist's Kingdom and power base will be in the Tribulation.

If indeed you believe Europe will be the seat of the Antichrist, with Europe and perhaps America being his power base, then I believe what is to follow may change your mind.

Firstly, the Antichrist not only has the Roman connection, he has Assyrian and Babylonian connections too. He will have Assyrian lineage or come from the peoples of the Assyrian Empire. Nimrod was called Asshur, which from the Hebrew root word 'Gaber' means 'strength, one 'who confirms a covenant' Gen 10:11. Nimrod built cities in what became known as Babylon, so he has Babylonian roots or will come from the peoples of the Babylonian empire. Revelation: 14: 3-4

Other scriptures confirming the Assyrian (read Babylonian) connection: Isaiah 10:5 ; 10: 12-14 ; 10: 25 ; 14:25 ; 30:31 ; 31:8 and a very clear indication of him being from the Assyrian people is Micah 5: 2-6 and 7:7

So, how can this be? How can this man be a Western European Roman, like the Pope, but still have ties, confirmed in scripture, to the Assyrian/Babylonian empires? Many have speculated that he will be a middle-eastern man that is now living in Europe or that he will form a confederation with the Roman Catholic Church that oversees a billion or more people, by actually moving to Rome.

But the Bible, really, is very simple if you study it enough. If this man has more than one lineage in his bloodline then it is safe to say that if you take a map of those various empires and overlap them, you will quickly determine that the Antichrist will come from a middle-eastern country and that he will not have to live in Europe at all to have a massive power base at his disposal. Assyria, you see, did not conquer Europe, but conquered land to its east and south and similarly the eastern leg of the Roman empire, which lasted 1000 years longer than the Western Roman Empire, became known as the Byzantine empire and it again had conquests to the east and south of Constantinople.

If you get a transparent copy of each map and overlay them, you will find that only 5 countries have a common geographical area that will support the place of birth for the Antichrist, as his 'coming from' a nation means he must be born there, not so? You will quickly determine that the five countries that are in the overlap of all of them are Egypt, Israel, Jordan, Lebanon and Syria. As discussed earlier, one of these nations will support the 8th King who is from one of ten nations, being the 11th King.

The excitement over the ten countries in the EU has distracted scholars for decades, but here in front of us are another ten countries that have been formed since the beginning of the last century. All of these countries are incorporated in the 7 empires of John's vision and the 5 empires of Daniel's vision.

10 modern-day countries that have arisen and are 'of' the previous 7 kingdoms. Revelation 17:7-11

- 1906 IRAN
- 1921 AFGHANISTAN
- 1922 EGYPT
- 1922 IRAQ
- 1924 TURKEY
- 1930 LEBANON
- 1938 SYRIA
- 1946 JORDAN
- 1947 PAKISTAN
- 1948 ISRAEL

However, NO European country is in the overlap of the empires discussed which means the Antichrist is not European. Remember, the Bible is an eastern book so it would stretch the imagination that God would use nations in ancient visions that no-one in their day knew anything about. Apart from trading with the coastal lands of Europe, the inner continent remained a dark mystery to the lands of the Bible until the Romans brought knowledge of it with them.

Iraq and Syria are part of ancient Assyria. We have already seen from previous scriptures that the Antichrist is referred to as the 'Assyrian'. He also has to come from the peoples of the other 7 kingdoms, which is possible if he comes from any one of the five nations listed above.

But which one?

I believe the key is the nation that is new (it springs up from the old, historical nations), being the small horn of the 11th King and there is only one country of the five that is a new nation without historically being an empire or nation of its own prior to 1946 and that country is Jordan. I surmise therefore, that the Antichrist will be Jordanian. The fact that he comes from a small horn with no real power supports this idea. However, there are other reasons that support this viewpoint.

- It fits the new horn prophecy. It is the only new country that has come out of all seven empires. All the others are ancient lands, including Lebanon which was the ancient Phoenician empire.
- The Jordanian Royal family are Hashemites. Hashem in Hebrew means 'the name' and Satan indwells the Antichrist to blaspheme 'THE' name (God).
- The Hashemites ruled Iraq (province of Assyria) for 37 years, ending with King Faisal's assassination in July 1958. The link to Babylon is thus established.
- Jews have called the Jordanian King the 'Prince of Jerusalem'.
- Jordan controls the temple mount through the Waqf and would therefore be in a leading position to grant Jewish sacrifices once more. Remember, the Jews will turn back to God in a big way after Ezekiel 38 but many will do so through Old Testament worship and practices. Permission would be needed from Jordan.
- Jordan already has a covenant with Israel. Daniel 9:27 says the Antichrist confirms a covenant with Israel. Only the King James Bible and one or two other translations use the word 'confirm'. The rest are possibly in error by saying he 'makes' a covenant. Making a covenant and confirming one are two different things. Therefore a sure sign of knowing who the Antichrist is, is the person confirming an existing covenant.
- Edom and Moab (Jordan) are spared in the wars with the Antichrist. It begs the question why? Dan 11:41
- Jews flee to South Jordan to escape the Antichrist where the Archangel Michael protects and nourishes them.
- Jordan is small and without power which supports previous scriptures we have discussed.
- A curiosity is that Rome, Jerusalem, Amman (capital of Jordan), Mecca and Tehran all sit on 7 hills (Revelation 17).
- Amman is a 'global city' which is becoming important in the global economic system.

Edom – southern Jordan; known as Edom, the place occupied by Esau, was and is a fierce enemy of Israel. The Palestinians are essentially Edomites. (Read the book of Obadiah). It stands to reason that an ancient enemy could provide the Antichrist.

Now, just because I say the Antichrist may be Jordanian does not mean I think he will be a Hashemite King (as the current King is) but may well be a new leader that rises up out of the ashes of the Psalm 83 war. It is interesting to note that Jordan is an enemy of Israel in the Psalm 83 conflict, which means there may be an imminent regime change about to happen in Jordan or that very strong Salafist, Al Qaeda, ISIS and Muslim Brotherhood forces operate from Jordanian territory, thus side-lining the Jordanian army and its King.

I do not say either, that the Antichrist will rule from Jordan and in fact, if the Bible is taken literally, as it should be, he should rule from Babylon.

Here are some other interesting facts about the Antichrist:

- He will have a 'stout' or fierce appearance. Daniel 7:20
- He will be older rather than younger and will have military knowledge (Alluded to by word stout)
- He will be deceitful and will understand mysteries. Dan 8:25 (This is very important and will be covered in later chapters).
- He will be a peacemaker Dan 11: 21-24 and Daniel 8:25 (He will kill in this 'peace' ... gas chambers? Another holocaust?)
- He will probably be secular, not holding to the God of his fathers
- He will be similar to other Antichrists like Nimrod, Antiochus Epiphanes and the Herodian Kings in character and intent.

Chapter 6

The 7 year Tribulation – also known as Daniel's 70th week

a) The first three and a half years after the Ezekiel 38 'war'

It must be remembered that as the Ezekiel 'war' ends, the people of Israel will have been convinced that God rescued them and will turn back to Him in great worship. Some Jews will do this in the old testament way and others will accept Christ as their redeemer. Millions of borderline 'believers' and people previously unconvinced that God even exists, will turn to Christ. For the purpose of the next few pages, I want to focus on the Jews that turn back to God to worship him in an old-testament fashion. To do this they need a temple and a red Heifer. They also need permission from the Waqf of Jerusalem or indeed the newly revealed Antichrist himself giving the 'nod' to rebuild their temple.

According to Prophecies in Daniel 9:27, Matthew 24:15 and 2 Thessalonians 2:4, a Temple will exist in Israel at the beginning of the Great Tribulation. This is confirmed by Revelation 11:1 which describes John measuring a Temple during the Tribulation. Its location is the 'Holy City.' Chapter 11 also introduces the two witnesses who preach in the 'Great City' and are ultimately killed there, their bodies left lying in the street. The Great City is identified as the place where the Lord was crucified: Jerusalem. But is Jerusalem also the Holy City?

According to Zechariah 14:6-9 on the day of the Lord's return (at the end of the Great Tribulation) an earthquake will split the Mount of Olives in two along an East-West line that creates a great valley through the centre of Jerusalem. Immediately a river will fill the valley creating a waterway from the Mediterranean to the Dead Sea. If the Lord returns to the same area of the Mount of Olives from which He left, as suggested by Acts 1:11, the earthquake creating this East-West valley will destroy the current Temple mount and anything that may be standing upon it.

Ezekiel 47:1-12 describes a great river flowing south from under the south side of the Temple and then eastward to the Dead Sea during a period of time that most scholars believe has not occurred yet. Revelation 22:1-2 confirms this. If as it appears, Ezekiel, Zechariah, and Revelation all describe the same river, then an interesting scenario begins to emerge. This scenario requires a Temple to be present on the day the Lord returns, but since the current Temple mount will have been destroyed by the earthquake mentioned above, this Temple must be somewhere else. Since the river originates under the Temple and flows from its south side before heading East and West, the Temple must be north of the newly created river valley.

Where Are The 12 Tribes?
Plotting the land grants for the 12 tribes given in the 48th chapter of Ezekiel on a map of Israel places the precincts of the Holy City somewhat north of the current City of Jerusalem. This new location is possibly the ancient City of Shiloh, where the Tabernacle stood for nearly 400 years after the Israelites first conquered the Land. This is the Holy City and its name is Jehovah Shammah according to the last verse in Ezekiel. The Hebrew translates as 'the LORD is here.' If accurate, this location would meet all the requirements for the Temple mentioned in the above references. The current Temple Mount in Jerusalem would not.

According to Ezekiel 44:6-9, this Temple will have been defiled in a way never seen in history, therefore at a time yet future to us. A foreigner uncircumcised in heart (neither Christian) and flesh (nor Jewish) will have been given charge of the sanctuary while offering sacrifices. If we understand the chronology of Ezekiel, this event will have taken place after both the 1948 re-gathering prophesied in Ezekiel 36-37 and the national wake-up call prophesied in Ezekiel 38-39 but before the Millennial Kingdom begins. The only event we know of that fits that chronology is the Great Tribulation. This is confirmed by Paul's prophecy of 2 Thessalonians 2:4 where the Antichrist sets himself up in the Temple proclaiming himself to be God.

Here then is a rough outline of events. Following Israel's return to God after the battle of Ezekiel 38-39, the Jewish people will re-establish their covenant (old not new) with Him. This will require a return to Levitical practices and so a Temple will be built. This is the Temple spoken of by Daniel, and John in Revelation. Following instructions given by Ezekiel and needing to avoid the enormous problems a Jerusalem Temple would create in the Moslem world, this Temple will possibly be located north of Jerusalem in

Shiloh. It will be defiled in the middle of the last 7 years as outlined in Daniel 9:24-27, Ezekiel 44:6-9, Matthew 24:15 and 2 Thessalonians 2:4 kicking off the Great Tribulation, but will be cleansed by living water that begins flowing on the day the Lord returns (Zechariah 14:8). This temple will be used during the Millennium to memorialise the Lord's work at the cross and provide the perspective for children born during the Kingdom Age to choose salvation just as you and I have had the perspective of the Lord's Supper in making our choice. Remember, He said, 'Do this in memory of Me until I come.' Acts 15:14-16 confirms that after the Lord has chosen a people from among the gentiles for Himself (the church) He will return and re-build David's fallen Tabernacle (the Temple). This is the Millennial Temple so vividly described in Ezekiel 40-48.

The New Jerusalem

The Ezekiel passage also solves the Jerusalem / New Jerusalem problem. For as long as I have been studying these things, there has been debate over the issue of the New Jerusalem. Some wonder how the Lord could permit redeemed believers and non- believing natural humans to co-exist in the Millennium. (The rotten apple spoiling the barrel theory) Others wonder how a city with a foot print 1400 miles square and tall could be located in Israel when the whole country won't be that big.

Carefully examining Revelation 21 and 22, we notice that John never actually says the city arrives on Earth. We are only told he sees it coming down out of Heaven, prepared as a bride. (Not that the city IS the bride, but that as with a bride on her wedding day, no effort has been spared to make it look its absolute best.)

I don't believe the city ever rests on the Earth's surface, but rather orbits in the proximity of Earth, like a satellite or perhaps another moon. Also, comparing the descriptions of New Jerusalem with Jehovah Shammah we see some similarities but enough differences to refute the notion that John and Ezekiel described the same place. Compare the following:

New Jerusalem (All verses from Revelation)	Jehovah Shammah (All verses from Ezekiel)
12 gates named after Israel (21:12)	12 gates named after Israel (48:30)
12 foundations named after Apostles (21:14)	Foundation not described

1400 miles square and tall (21:16)	One mile square (48:30)
Coming Down from Heaven (21:2)	Located in Israel on Earth (40:2)
No Temple ... God and the Lamb are its Temple (21:22)	Temple just north of the city (40:2)
No sin; nothing impure will ever enter (21:27)	Daily sin offerings in the Temple (45:13-15,17)
No more death (21:4)	Still death (44:25 also Isa 65:20)
No natural beings ... only the perfected (21:27)	Natural Beings (46:16)

With the differentiation of these two Holy Cities, the apparent conflict between Jewish and Christian eschatology is resolved. Israel was promised that one day GOD would come to Earth to dwell among them forever, while the Church is promised that Jesus will come to take us to Heaven to live with Him there. Both promises come true.

Since Ezekiel specifically quoted the Lord's promise to dwell among the Israelites Revelation (43:7) and then described the new Holy City, while Jesus promised to return for the Church to take us to be with Him (John 14:1-3), they must have been talking about two different destinations. They were. Heaven is where the New Jerusalem exits from, where we will dwell with the Lord forever, while the Holy City on Earth is Jehovah Shammah where God will dwell in the midst of His people Israel forever.

The red Heifer

The Lord said to Moses and Aaron: 'This is a requirement of the law that the Lord has commanded: Tell the Israelites to bring you a red heifer without defect or blemish and that has never been under a yoke. Give it to Eleazar the priest; it is to be taken outside the camp and slaughtered in his presence. Then Eleazar the priest is to take some of its blood on his finger and sprinkle it seven times toward the front of the tent of meeting. While he watches, the heifer is to be burned—its hide, flesh, blood and intestines. The priest is to take some cedar wood, hyssop and scarlet wool and throw them onto the burning heifer' (Numbers 19:1-6).

For the first time in several years there has been a report (in 2018) of a red heifer being born. (Actually it's a red calf, since a heifer is a young cow at least a year old which has not had a calf of her own.) This has caused a stir in Orthodox Jewish circles as well as among prophecy conscious Christians. The reason being that the ashes of a pure red heifer are an essential ingredient in the purification water necessary to restore the Jewish people to ceremonial cleanliness. Unclean people cannot build and worship in a holy Temple, and a Temple is necessary to fulfil end times prophecy.

Therefore the appearance of a red heifer is a sign that one of the last requirements for the construction of a Temple could soon be met. Notice I said could be met. I have already seen several news reports and articles that act as if Temple construction could begin tomorrow. But the truth is that it will be three years before the heifer is old enough and during that time if it should sprout as few as two (2) non red hairs it will be disqualified.

A pure red heifer is a rare animal. Even its hooves have to be red. In all the history of Israel only nine red heifers have been sacrificed, the last one about 2,000 years ago in 15 AD. The Great Hebrew sage Maimonides (1135-1204 AD) claimed that the 10th red heifer would herald the coming of the Messiah.

After All This Time?
After 15 AD There's no record of a potential red heifer being born until the mid 1990's when one was born through a special program conducted jointly by breeders in the USA and the Temple Institute in Jerusalem. I remember the excitement it caused among students of prophecy and was blessed to be able to discuss this with both the American and the Jewish overseers of the breeding programme at a meeting I hosted for them in 1994. It was one of a series of meetings they were conducting in the USA to increase awareness among Christians of their effort to raise a qualified red heifer.

I had first met Rabbi Chaim Richman, who was representing the Temple Institute, a few years earlier during my first trip to Israel. He is one of the world's leading authorities on the red heifer, and much of the material that follows came from his book on the subject that he kindly gave to me during that visit to the US.

Excitement was running high until 4 white hairs were found in the heifer's tail. Since then there have been a few other candidates, but all have been similarly disqualified. Like the others, this current calf will have to remain 100% red for 3 years to qualify. All sacrifices to the Lord have to be free from any defect, spot, or blemish, but you might wonder why this heifer has to be 100% red. According to Rabbi Richman, it's explained in Isaiah 1:18, *'Come now let us reason together,' says the Lord. 'Though your sins are like scarlet they shall be white as snow. Though they are red as crimson they shall be as wool.'*

God is not approximate about anything. If the heifer is supposed to be red, it has to be 100% red, because that's the way God sees things. For example, to be sin free we can't just be pretty good, we have to be perfect. The presence of any sins in our life, even little ones, makes us sinners through and through. For sins no greater by comparison than a couple of non red hairs on a red cow we are excluded from the presence of God. James said the violation of even one law makes us guilty of all (James 2:10). Get the idea?

When the red heifer is completely burned its ashes are white. Being mixed together with pure water from a spring or a brook (called living water) and sprinkled on the people purifies them from their sins (a foreshadow of Christ's blood, red, washing sins away to make one as pure and white as snow).

But like all the remedies for sin in the Old Covenant the ashes of the red heifer only cleansed them from the sins of the past. It gave them no protection going forward. Every time they sinned, the sacrifices and rituals had to be repeated. Since they could never stop sinning, they could never stop sacrificing. This is one of the primary differences between the Old Covenant and our version of the New Covenant. The writer of Hebrews explained that the same sacrifices repeated endlessly year after year could never make perfect those who drew near to worship (Hebrews 10:1). But when Jesus offered for all time one sacrifice for sin, He made perfect forever we who are being made holy (Hebrews 10:12-14).

Reading The Fine Print
'A man who is clean shall gather up the ashes of the heifer and put them in a ceremonially clean place outside the camp. They are to be kept by the Israelite community for use in the water of cleansing; it is for purification from sin' (Numbers 19:9).

But the red heifer alone won't guarantee that Temple construction can begin. The verse above tells us that in addition to the priest who supervises this, someone who is ritually clean has to be responsible for collecting and storing the ashes.

Normally ashes from previous red heifers would be used to qualify someone for this job. In Biblical times ashes from all of the previous heifers were stored at the Temple. These ashes were undoubtedly preserved in advance of the second Temple's destruction because of their importance. But over the last 2,000 years the location of the preserved ashes has been lost. Most experts think they are probably in the same area of Qumran where the Dead Sea Scrolls were discovered. Over the years, numerous searches have been made there using the latest technology, but to date they remain undiscovered. If an unclean person gathers up the ashes, it would make the entire supply unclean, so they must find a way to purify a man to gather up the ashes of the new sacrifice and see that they are properly stored.

Then there's the issue of obtaining pure water to mix with the ashes. Again, only someone who is ritually clean can collect the water. In Temple times the water was obtained at the spring that fed the pool of Siloam. An ingenious method was implemented to assure the water was not accidentally made unclean in the process of obtaining it.

Jewish people believe they can become unclean by coming in contact with a dead body. Since the creation so many people and animals have died and been buried or simply left to decay that to them the ground itself is a source of uncleanness. Because of this the Temple is built atop a foundation consisting of a series of alternating arches extending down to bedrock to insure it can't ever become unclean.

The water from the spring comes out of the Earth pure. To be sure it stayed that way, certain pregnant women were selected to give birth in a special facility built to guarantee there was no possibility that the children they brought into the world could inadvertently be made unclean. The children were raised in purity in this sequestered environment until they reached eight years of age when they were pronounced ready to obtain the water.

Riding on boards attached to oxen so as not to come into contact with the ground, they were taken down to the spring to collect the water and bring it back up to the temple. Arriving there they mixed the water with ashes from previous heifers and sprinkled the priest who would conduct the sacrifice of the next heifer. The priest would then walk across a special bridge that was built atop a series of arches from the Temple mount across the Kidron valley to the Mt. of Olives where the altar upon which the red heifer was sacrificed was located.

(The Mt. Of Olives is where the red heifer was sacrificed, in the upper right hand corner with the bridge that connected it to the East Gate of the Temple. The offset arches that prevented anything from the ground below from contaminating the pavement upon which the priest walked, allowing him to remain ritually pure.) [Author – all those rituals to become saved versus accepting Christ as your saviour, which is one act! Which would you choose?]

Of course, Temple Institute officials know all this, and are preparing to meet these requirements, even though they can't do so today. So in spite of the breathless headlines proclaiming that the requirements for building the third Temple have now been met, the facts tell a different story. Now don't get me wrong, the appearance of another red heifer candidate is big news, and it could turn out to be one more of the many signs we see around us that we're in the end of the end times. But it does not mean that all the hurdles have been cleared for building the next Temple. Far from it.

Probably the biggest hurdle is the desire of the Jewish people themselves. Currently most of those who are pushing for a Temple are doing so for the wrong reason. They think building a Temple will prove to the world that the 'Palestinians' are wrong when they insist the Jews have no historical connection to Jerusalem. To these people, having a Temple there would be a huge political victory. The problem is that alone would not bring the nation any closer to God. Those who want a Temple to renew their covenant with Him are still in the minority.

What is it going to take?

I believe it will take the Battle of Ezekiel 38 with the supernatural victory God will win for them to ignite a true national desire to come back to Him, and that's when they will become serious about building a Temple. In Ezekiel 39:21-22 the Lord said,

'I will display my glory among the nations, and all the nations will see the punishment I inflict and the hand I lay on them. From that day forward the people of Israel will know that I am the Lord their God.'

And even then they'll be fooled into thinking the Antichrist is their Messiah, and will let him defile their new Temple. Daniel prophesied that this will happen.

'He will confirm a covenant with many for one 'seven.' In the middle of the 'seven' he will put an end to sacrifice and offering. And at the temple he will set up an abomination that causes desolation, until the end that is decreed is poured out on him' (Daniel 9:27)

Speaking of the same event, Paul said,

He will oppose and will exalt himself over everything that is called God or is worshiped, so that he sets himself up in God's temple, proclaiming himself to be God (2 Thessalonians 2:4).

And when God returns to dwell in the Temple during the millennium, one of His first statements will be to accuse Israel of letting this happen.

'In addition to all your other detestable practices, you brought foreigners uncircumcised in heart and flesh into my sanctuary, desecrating my temple while you offered me food, fat and blood, and you broke my covenant. Instead of carrying out your duty in regard to my holy things, you put others in charge of my sanctuary' (Ezekiel 44:7-8).

You have Got The Wrong Guy

As Christians we believe the construction of the Temple will precede the coming of the Messiah. Daniel (Daniel 9:27), Jesus (Matthew 24:15-21), Paul (2 Thessalonians 2:4), and John (Revelation 11:1) all confirm this. Therefore the one Israel will welcome as the Messiah who will help them build the Temple, will in fact be the Antichrist. Speaking to Israel, Jesus said, *'I have come in my father's name and you do not accept me. But if someone else comes in his own name, you will accept him'* (John 5:43). And so it will be.

Even so, the birth of a calf that could become the 10th red heifer is important news for Israel and for prophecy students everywhere. For Israel it could mean that the coming of the Messiah is close, although the time before He comes will include the Great Tribulation. For the Church it could be one more sign that the Rapture is even closer.

More and more prophecy scholars are agreeing that what's unique about our time is not that there are specific signs telling us we're at the end of the age. What's unique is that all the signs we were told to look for are here *now!*

~※ ₢~

So, although the Jews will be given their new temple to worship in and many in the world will see the Antichrist as some type of messiah after his peace treaty victory, the world will quickly descend into war as the Antichrist rises to power and authority over them, no doubt juggling with each other for his political and economic favour.

~※ ₢~

He will be disguised as a peacemaker and will fool much of the world at first. But with the arrival of the red horse (2nd seal) his real intent will become clear.

1 Thessalonians 5:3 tells us while people are saying peace and safety destruction will come upon them suddenly. I think this means just as people

have begun to believe that the Antichrist's resolution of the Battle of Ezekiel 38 is working, war will break out again. But I don't believe the world will suddenly sink into a state of anarchy with countries attacking each other on their own initiative. I think the Antichrist will be orchestrating this and will convince people that these wars are necessary to bring a lasting peace.

And remember, the Russians will be defeated in Ezekiel's battle and some say their homeland will sustain nuclear attacks during that time as well (Ezekiel 39:6). They may not be in any shape to mount another attack on anyone so soon afterward.

The Seal, Trumpet and Bowl Judgements

The combination of the Rapture and the Battle of Ezekiel 38 will fill the world with anguish and uncertainty as Daniel's 70th Week begins. Where did all those people go? How did Israel so utterly destroy that massive invasion force all by 'itself'? How did all these things happen so suddenly? Why didn't somebody see this coming and do something to prevent it?

The Seal Judgments

In the midst of all the chaos and confusion one leader will stand out (Revelation 6:2). He will demonstrate an incredible ability to restore the world's hope for the future, and promise to bring them peace. The frightened populace will easily be persuaded to follow his lead. He will agree to Israel's demand for a Temple in which to resume their long abandoned worship of the One who had secured their victory. He will do this, not because He wants to help them honour God, but because he has plans of his own for the Temple (Daniel 9:27, 2 Thessalonians 2:4).

Using their own Scriptures (Ezekiel 48:1-10) he will show Israel why their new Temple should not be built where the old ones had stood. Instead it should be located a few miles north, in ancient Shiloh, where the Tabernacle had once stood. This will leave the Muslim facilities on the current Temple mount intact, at least for a time. After the disappearance of the Church, Islam will fast become the dominant religion of the world and their third holiest place is on that mount. With this bold stroke he will bring a semblance of peace to the region, demonstrating that Jew and Muslim can live in peace as neighbours in his brave new world (Daniel 8:25). The people of Earth will breathe a collective sigh of relief. But all too soon wars will start to break out in various places (Revelation 6:3) because this leader's ultimate goal is world domination and some nations will resist. He'll convince people that war is a temporary but necessary inconvenience and assure them that everything will soon be all right again. But the combination of wars, food shortages, and runaway inflation will begin taking their toll (Revelation 6:6). The deadly effects of this combination will be felt across one fourth of the Earth (Revelation 6:8).

Though it's often called a religion of peace, Islam offers the world only two options, submission or death, as the martyrs among believers of other faiths will soon learn. For the multitude of new Christians who witnessed the disappearance of friends and family in the Rapture and know from first hand experience the truth of the gospel, conversion to Islam will be impossible and the number of those who will die for their faith will mount rapidly and steadily. (Revelation 6:9) They will cry out to the Lord for vengeance but He will caution them to be patient for a little while longer because many more will die just as they have (Revelation 6:10-11).

Without warning, a great earthquake that will be felt world wide will trigger volcanic action spewing millions of tons of ash into the air, blotting out the Sun and making the Moon turn blood red (Revelation 6:12-14). The world's leaders will run for cover, some intuitively knowing that the Wrath of God they were warned about by the Christians who have all disappeared has already begun and they will be shown no quarter. (Revelation 6:16-17)

The Trumpet Judgments

As if to confirm the worst fears of these leaders, a storm of hail, fire, and blood will rain down upon the Earth burning up a third of it. A third of the trees and all the green grass will go up in smoke (Revelation 8:7) A meteor-like object the size of a huge mountain will crash into the sea. The resulting contamination will turn a third of the world's oceans to blood killing all the marine life in the affected areas. The tsunami this meteor causes will capsize and destroy a third of the ships in the world. Over 15,000 commercial ships will disappear in a single day (Revelation 8:8-9). Then another star will fall to Earth and when it does a third of the fresh water will be contaminated. It will be toxic and foul tasting and many people will die from drinking it (Revelation 8:10-11). Both the day and the night will lose a third of their light due to the smoke and ash from the fires and volcanoes. Through the choking haze an angelic messenger will bring a warning from the Lord, 'The worst is yet to come.' (Revelation 8:12-13). A fallen angel will open the shaft of the

Abyss and smoke will billow forth, further contaminating the already toxic air. Creatures resembling locusts will fly out from the smoke and for 5 months will inflict scorpion like stings on the people. These stings will be so painful people will wish they could die, but there will be no escape (Revelation 9:1-11). The only people on Earth who will be immune to their venom will be the 144,000 evangelists the Lord will have commissioned from among the tribes of Israel (Revelation 7:1-8).

Four angels who have been bound at the gateway to the East (the Euphrates River) will be released to kill one third of the Earth's remaining population with plagues of fire, smoke and Sulphur. (Revelation 9:13-19). The East is far different from the West and the animosity between Muslims, Hindus, Buddhists, and other religions of the Far East is well established and deadly. Since 40% of the world's population is crowded into the nations east of the Euphrates the number of casualties will be enormous as they fight each other for supremacy.

Between the Rapture, the martyrdom, the wars and the judgments, well over two billion people will no longer be found among the living on planet Earth as Daniel's 70th Week approaches the mid point. And yet the Bible gives no indication that the unbelievers who remain will see the error of their ways and change their minds. This is the hardest core of the unsaved, the ones who refused to believe the truth of the Lord and accepted the lie of the Antichrist instead (2 Thessalonians 2:10). In their deluded state they will think they are on the side of light not darkness, and right not wrong. They will see God as the invading enemy and Satan as their leader, working to protect them. Spiritually, everything will be upside down.

But at the blowing of the 7th Trumpet in Heaven, the Lord's reign will begin (Revelation 11:15). Having used every device at His command in an effort to persuade the people of Earth to change their minds and accept His offer of pardon, He will now take action to unseat the usurper from the throne that's rightfully His and claim for Himself that which He's purchased with His own blood, Planet Earth. Those who have sided with Satan will now face the worst time of judgment in the history of mankind. Were it not for a remnant of the Lord's people among them, not a single soul would be left standing when this is over (Matthew 24:21-22).

The Bowl Judgments

The Bowl judgments make up the three and half year period of time we know as the Great Tribulation. The Seal and Trumpet cycles of judgments (1st 3 ½ years) were partly for the purpose of demonstrating evidence of God's existence to the undecided among the people of Earth. But that will have come to an end with the Bowl judgments. They're strictly for the purpose of bringing judgment upon those who have rejected Him. In the process the Lord is going to completely destroy all the nations to which His people have been scattered (Jeremiah 30:11). Today there are nearly as many Jews in America as there are in Israel, and more than there are in any other nation, so you know that what's left of this country after the Rapture will not escape.

By now Satan will have been expelled from Heaven (Revelation 12:9) and confined to Earth (Revelation 12:13). He will unleash his full fury upon God's people. But those Jews who heed His warning (Matthew 24:15-21) will be escorted to a place of refuge in Petra, out of Satan's reach (Revelation 12:13-16). Enraged, he will turn his fury against the Gentiles who have come to believe Jesus is their Saviour since the Rapture (Revelation 12:17).

He will take up residence in the body of the Antichrist (Revelation 13:4) and with the help of a false prophet he will convince the unbelieving world to follow him and take a mark on their right hand or forehead to prove their loyalty to him (Revelation 13:16-17).

Three angels will deliver God's final messages to mankind. The first one will offer one last chance to accept the Gospel, the second will announce the coming destruction of Babylon and all the city represents, and the third will warn mankind against taking the mark of the beast. (Revelation 14:6-11)

People who disregard the warning against taking the mark will be treated to a dose of ugly and painful sores (Revelation 16:2). All the water on Earth will turn to blood, whether in the sea (Revelation 16:3) or in springs and rivers (Revelation 16:4). All sources of water will now be contaminated. The angel in charge of the waters reminds us that God is just in doing this because those He's judging have shed the blood of God's saints and prophets. Now He's giving them blood to drink. (Revelation 16:5-7). The Sun will go super nova at this point becoming so hot people will be scorched just by going outside. Again they will curse God but refuse to repent. (Revelation 16:8-9).Then the Sun will go totally dark turning day into night, and still the people of Earth will curse God but refuse to repent (Revelation 16:10-11).

The Antichrist will gather the armies of the world to Armageddon in a final effort to repel the Earth's 'invaders'. [Author – Society, backed by Hollywood and non Christian religions and scientists/new age believers will see Christ and Christians as evil people, invaders of the planet Earth, preventing Mother Earth and its children to move forward in the next leap of evolution]. From Heaven a loud voice will shout, 'It is done!' and the full fury of God's wrath will be loosed on Earth. Lightning, thunder, and the worst earthquake man has ever experienced will be followed by a torrent of 100 pound hail stones. (Revelation 16:17-21) The punishment for blasphemy is stoning, and the blaspheming people of Earth will suffer the most extreme form of this punishment for their behaviour.

Babylon The Great

Then God will turn to Babylon, headquarters of the forces who have defied Him since the time after the flood. There are three components to mankind's world-wide system and they will all be headquartered there. They are governmental, commercial, and religious, and among them they have enslaved the people of Earth for thousands of years. First God will use the governmental component to destroy the religious one.

'The beast (Antichrist) *and the ten horns* (ten kings who assist him) *you saw will hate the prostitute* (religious ecumenical Babylon – 'Chrislam'). *They will bring her to ruin and leave her naked; they will eat her flesh and burn her with fire. For God has put it into their hearts to accomplish his purpose by agreeing to give the beast their power to rule, until God's words are fulfilled.'* (Revelation 17:16-17)

Then He will turn to the commercial component. It will be so totally destroyed that Earth's leaders will stand aghast, scarcely believing what their own eyes are telling them.

They will weep and mourn and cry out, 'Woe! Woe, O great city, dressed in fine linen, purple and scarlet, and glittering with gold, precious stones and pearls! In one hour such great wealth has been brought to ruin!' (Revelation 18:16-17)

Finally the governmental component.

The beast was captured, and with him the false prophet who had performed the miraculous signs on his behalf. With these signs he had deluded those who had received the mark of the beast and worshiped his image. The two of them were thrown alive into the fiery lake of burning sulphur. The rest of them were killed with the sword that came out of the mouth of the rider on the horse, and all the birds gorged themselves on their flesh. (Revelation 19:20-21)

For six thousand years God has worked tirelessly to reconcile man to Himself, even giving His own life in exchange for ours. But His efforts have all ended in failure due to mankind's unfaithfulness. Covenant after covenant was instituted and broken. The only one that has endured is the one the Father made with His Son to save us. But even then the majority of mankind, given the choice to participate as a beneficiary in this everlasting covenant, refused. Soon, His patience exhausted, God will remove the remnant that chose the pardon He offers, and judge the rest. Can you blame Him?

b) The Great Tribulation
The Great Tribulation (last 3 ½ years) is about to begin on Earth. The Temple will soon be made desolate. When that happens, the Jewish remnant will heed the Lord's call from Matthew 24:15-16 and flee to a place of supernatural protection as we saw in Revelation 12. When they do, Satan's target of opportunity will become the so-called Tribulation Saints, those who have come to faith in the Lord after the Rapture. One of the Antichrist's first goals after proclaiming himself to be God and setting up his counterfeit religion will be to shut down this new movement of God's. Since they're scattered all over the place the best way to do that is to freeze them out of the economy, making it impossible for them to earn wages or buy life's essentials.

While discussing Job, Satan had chided God, 'He only worships you because you bless him and protect him. Take it all away and he will curse you.'(Job 1:9-11) Now he has his man, the Antichrist, go after the Tribulation Saints the same way. Deprive them of enough and these new converts will either turn or die. Either way, he will soon be rid of them, or so he thinks.

Revelation 13
And the dragon stood on the shore of the sea. (Revelation 13:1)

Having been cast out of Heaven, Satan stands by the sea, a euphemism for the gentile nations (Daniel 7:2) ready to do his worst on Planet Earth.

The Beast Out Of The Sea
And I saw a beast coming out of the sea. He had ten horns and seven heads, with ten crowns on his horns, and on each head a blasphemous name. The beast I saw resembled a leopard, but had feet like those of a bear and a mouth like that of a lion. The dragon gave the beast his power and his throne and great authority. One of the heads of the beast seemed to have had a fatal wound, but the fatal

wound had been healed. The whole world was astonished and followed the beast. Men worshiped the dragon because he had given authority to the beast, and they also worshiped the beast and asked, 'Who is like the beast? Who can make war against him?'(Revelation 13:2-4)

As the same beasts in Daniel 7:1-7 represented Babylon (lion) Persia (bear) and Greece (leopard) it makes sense to see them that way here. The order is reversed because Daniel was looking forward in time while John was looking back. When Daniel saw Rome, he could not compare it to any animal he had seen, so he called it a large and terrifying beast. John shows it to be a monster with multiple heads and horns.

But the personal pronouns in John's description indicate a king rather than a kingdom. That means that the speed of Alexander (the leopard), the strength of Cyrus (the bear), and the boastful roar of Nebuchadnezzar (the lion) are all present in this king. And what's more, he wields all the power and authority of Satan, even seating himself on Satan's throne. This monster in the guise of a man is the Antichrist, finally revealing his true nature. Having complete power (10 horns ; Possibly Russia/China/India and many other countries), supernatural wisdom (7 heads) and officially recognized as 'The' authority over all (10 crowns) he is set to make the world over in his own image, and those whose hearts are focused on the things of Earth are loving it. He's apparently come to power through a botched assassination attempt that's left his right eye blinded and his right arm withered (Zechariah 11:17). The world thought he had died, but here he is alive. Rumours of his resurrection add to his aura and are encouraged.

By the way, notice he comes out of the sea, symbolic of the Gentile nations, and that he has the dominant characteristics of the three most powerful Gentile Kings. John may be telling us that the Antichrist is a Gentile. And from Ezekiel 44:7-8 we learn he is not circumcised.

Confirmation?

The beast was given a mouth to utter proud words and blasphemies and to exercise his authority for forty-two months. He opened his mouth to blaspheme God, and to slander his name and his dwelling place and those who live in Heaven. He was given power to make war against the saints and to conquer them. And he was given authority over every tribe, people, language and nation. All inhabitants of the Earth will worship the beast—all whose names have not been written in the book of life belonging to the Lamb that was slain from the creation of the world. (Revelation 13:5-8)

The saints being conquered here can not be the Church, because Jesus promised that the gates of Hell would not overcome the Church (Matthew 16:18). In Biblical times the rulers or leaders of a city had their offices in the large structure that surrounded the main gates into the city. We can see evidence of this in the Books of Ruth (Ruth 4:1-2) and Esther (Esther 5:9). The gates came to symbolize the leaders. It's the same today when we say, 'You can't fight City Hall.' We are not referring to the building but to the officials who work there. The phrase gates of Hell is a euphemism for Satan.

Having consolidated his power over Earth, and endearing himself to the Jews by helping them build a Temple, the Antichrist now marches into the Holy City to stand in the Temple and declare that he's God in the flesh (2 Thessalonians 2:4), slandering His Name, making His House desolate, and mounting a full sale attack on remaining believers. Satan's boast the he would make himself like the Most High (Isaiah 14:14) got him kicked out of Heaven for good and marked the beginning of the Great Tribulation in Heaven. But on Earth it's different. People from every part of the Earth will worship Satan and the Antichrist. Jesus warned the believing remnant of Israel to flee into the mountains when they see this happening (Matthew. 24:15-16) saying it will signal the beginning of the Great Tribulation on Earth (Matthew. 24:21)

A more literal translation of Revelation 13: 8 reads, ' *and all who dwell on Earth will worship it (the beast), everyone whose name has not been written before the foundation of the world in the book of life of the Lamb that was slain.'* It's the version used by the New American Standard and the English Standard, two of the most literal translations of the Greek. It speaks clearly to the validity of the doctrine of Eternal Security. If you're saved, God knew about it before He created the Earth. Prior to giving Adam his first breath He looked down over the vast span of time and saw the moment when you would make your independent decision to serve Him. (He foreknew.) And that's when He made a reservation for you in His Kingdom, swearing never to blot your name out of the book. (He predestined you to take on His Son's image.) When the time was right he spoke to your heart, knowing you'd respond. (He called.) And when you did He cleansed you from all of your sins, regarding you from that time forward as if you have never sinned at all. (He justified.) And one day soon He will give you a new eternal body and a place near Him in His Kingdom. (He glorified.) (Romans 8: 29-30)

In the context of time you made your own free choice to accept the pardon that Jesus purchased for you. But having seen the end from the beginning, He has always known that you would. All your life He's watched over you, preparing you for your day of decision. And ever since then He's protected you, for He promised He would never lose any of those He's been given. (John 6:39-40) He knows that it's the shepherd's job to keep the sheep. And He's the Good Shepherd.

'He who has an ear, let him hear. If anyone is to go into captivity, into captivity he will go. If anyone is to be killed with the sword, with the sword he will be killed. This calls for patient endurance and faithfulness on the part of the saints' (Revelation 13:9–10).

Again we're told that the Great Tribulation will not be cut short, but will run the full three and a half years ordained for it from ancient times. Nor will anyone from this point on be miraculously preserved. The judgments will come and will run their course.

'Be faithful unto death,' He told the Church at Smyrna, *'And I will give you the crown of life.'* (Revelation 2:10) Like it was at the beginning of Christianity, so it will be at the end. The penalty for loving Jesus is death. Let me hasten to remind you that the Christian Era does not end with the Church. There will be Christians on Earth for several more years after the Church is gone.

The Beast Out Of The Earth

Then I saw another beast, coming out of the Earth. He had two horns like a lamb, but he spoke like a dragon. He exercised all the authority of the first beast on his behalf, and made the Earth and its inhabitants worship the first beast, whose fatal wound had been healed. And he performed great and miraculous signs, even causing fire to come down from Heaven to Earth in full view of men. Because of the signs he was given power to do on behalf of the first beast, he deceived the inhabitants of the Earth. He ordered them to set up an image in honour of the beast who was wounded by the sword and yet lived. He was given power to give breath to the image of the first beast, so that it could speak and cause all who refused to worship the image to be killed. He also forced everyone, small and great, rich and poor, free and slave, to receive a mark on his right hand or on his forehead, so that no one could buy or sell unless he had the mark, which is the name of the beast or the number of his name. (Revelation 13:11-17)

We call this second beast the False Prophet. The fact that he comes out of the Earth means that he's an ordinary man. Saying he has two horns like a lamb but speaks like a dragon means he's the religious authority for those who worship Satan. It's a counterfeit version of the relationship Jesus (the Lamb) had with His father (God). In John 8:28 Jesus said, *'I do nothing on my own but speak just what the Father has taught me.'* So it will be with the false prophet. He will speak only what Satan has taught him. He heads up the one world religion, and makes certain that it's united in its worship of the Antichrist. Building a great image of him, he uses supernatural power from Satan to give it a semblance of life (hologram??) and makes everyone worship it on pain of death. Because no one can tell if another person is really worshiping or just going through the motions, he devises a test. Those who are loyal to the Antichrist and truly worship him, must agree to take a mark to prove it. It will not only demonstrate their sincerity, but allow them to participate fully in mainstream life without fear. Refusing the mark means they have given their heart to Jesus. If they are caught, the penalty is death. And even if they are not, they will face a nearly impossible challenge in just staying alive (perhaps this is when survivalists who have stored food etc will come into their own, as believers of course).

'This calls for wisdom. If anyone has insight, let him calculate the number of the beast (Author – not the false prophet, but the Antichrist) *, for it is man's number. His number is 666'*. (Revelation 13:18)

This verse has been subject to much speculation and incorrect interpretation because it tells us so little. It says only that the Antichrist's number is the number of a man, and that his number is literally 600 and 60 and 6, which may be different from 666. We don't know.

What we do know is that both Biblical languages (Hebrew and Greek) gave numerical values to the letters of their alphabets to compensate for their lack of a direct numbering system. The Romans used Roman Numerals, assigning numerical values to a few letters, and today much of the world uses Hindu-Arabic Numerals, value specific symbols originally developed in the 2nd century BC but not widely used until several hundred years later. If (and it's a big if) the numbers six hundred, sixty, and six, are supposed to signify a name, then the numerical value of the Antichrist's name would probably have to equal that amount in its Greek form, Greek being the language of the Revelation.

I don't think it makes sense to devise a numerical equivalent for the letters of the English alphabet to figure this out because, outside of certain pagan religious practices, there's no accepted valuing system for doing so. We have always used Arabic numerals and so have not assigned numerical equivalents to the letters in our alphabet like the Hebrews, Greeks and, to a lesser extent, the Romans did. Some think that the number might apply to something other than his name, his birthday for instance, or a title of some sort. It could also be a registration number, like the American Social Security number, or any one of the other numbers by which we are known in various aspects of our lives.

The big qualifier for the verse is the phrase 'let him who has understanding.' To me that disqualifies most of us from even guessing. It seems that a person would have to have an understanding of the practice of Gematria, the calculation of the numerical equivalence of letters, words, or phrases in Biblical Greek to come up with the answer. [Author – I have recently read that this man's identity will only become obvious to the Tribulation Saints as they will know who the Antichrist is, while we won't as we will be in Heaven. It's best to put aside trying to figure out who he is for that reason].

Daniel 12:4 tells us that in the latter days knowledge will increase. That means that pretty soon someone will crack this code. Personally, I think it's unlikely that this will happen before the church disappears.

Revelation 14

The Lamb And The 144,000

'Then I looked, and there before me was the Lamb, standing on Mount Zion, and with him 144,000 who had his name and his Father's name written on their foreheads. And I heard a sound from Heaven like the roar of rushing waters and like a loud peal of thunder. The sound I heard was like that of harpists playing their harps. And they sang a new song before the throne and before the four living creatures and the elders. No one could learn the song except the 144,000 who had been redeemed from the Earth. These are those who did not defile themselves with women, for they kept themselves pure. They follow the Lamb wherever he goes. They were purchased from among men and offered as firstfruits to God and the Lamb. No lie was found in their mouths; they are blameless. (Revelation 14:1-5)

In Revelation 7 we saw that it makes sense to view the 144,000 there just as they're described … Messianic Jews from the 12 tribes of Israel, witnessing to the world after the church is gone. They are the end times fulfilment of the prophecy in Isaiah 43:10, being witnesses for the Lord to the nations of Earth during Daniel's 70th week.

Then Who Are These Guys?

Here, the same sized group, 144,000, is shown standing on Mt. Zion and they have the names of both the Father and the Son written on their foreheads. They are described as having been redeemed from the Earth and are before the Throne of God singing a new song, a song only they can sing. Hebrews 12:22-24 provides a beautiful description of this group. *'But you have come to Mt. Zion, to the Heavenly Jerusalem, the city of the Living God. You have come to thousands upon thousands of angels in joyful assembly, to the Church of the Firstborn whose names are written in Heaven. You have come to God, the judge of all men, to the spirits of righteous men made perfect, to Jesus the Mediator of a new covenant and to the sprinkled blood that speaks a better word than the blood of Abel.'* It was written to the Church.

The similarity is unmistakable. By their location (Heaven) their spiritual state (righteous men made perfect) and their dedication to both God and Jesus they are reminiscent of a group first seen in Revelation 5 and described as Kings and Priests. They sing a new song just like that group, they follow the Lamb wherever He goes, signifying that they're His disciples, and they were purchased from among men (1 Corinthians 6:19-20) and offered as first fruits to God and the Lamb.

Though it's tempting to see them as the original 144,000, martyred and in Heaven, only one group fits that description perfectly … the Church. This 144,000 is a sampling of the redeemed, brought to Heaven in the Rapture of Revelation 4, and presented as the first fruits of the harvest of souls, just as the wave offering was the first fruits of the harvest of grain (Lev. 23:9-14). All the grain was harvested, but only a sample was presented. So it is with the Church. The 144,000 is not meant to be the full number of Raptured believers, just a sample.

As far as the phrase 'defiled themselves with women' is concerned, it's used to symbolize the worship of idols. Since pagan worship was sexual in nature, the Lord sometimes described idol worship in sexual terms. (Read Ezekiel 16 & 23 if you dare.) These 144,000 had not done that. In fact they were found to be totally blameless, further evidence that they're the redeemed in Heaven. No human on Earth is blameless, and there's no Biblical evidence that men who remain celibate will receive special rewards.

The Three Angels

'Then I saw another angel flying in midair, and he had the eternal gospel to proclaim to those who live on the Earth—to every nation, tribe, language and people. He said in a loud voice, 'Fear God and give him glory, because the hour of his judgment has come. Worship him who made the Heavens, the Earth, the sea and the springs of water.' (Revelation 14:5-7)

Notice the tremendous contrast between the preceding view of things in Heaven and this warning of what's about to befall the Earth. It's the last warning before the dreaded Bowl Judgments that will soon come to complete, not begin, God's wrath.

In Matthew. 24:14 Jesus promised that the Gospel would be preached in all the nations before the end of the age. People have speculated on whether this angel is really satellite TV or something of that nature, but it does not matter. Between the first 144,000, the Tribulation believers, and this angel, His promise has been kept.

'A second angel followed and said, 'Fallen! Fallen is Babylon the Great, which made all the nations drink the maddening wine of her adulteries.' (Revelation 14:8). This verse speaks of the coming collapse of the one world church. As we'll see in Revelation 17, the Antichrist has used this 'church' as a means to an end. But now it's time for all the world to worship him and him alone.

'A third angel followed them and said in a loud voice: 'If anyone worships the beast and his image and receives his mark on the forehead or on the hand, he, too, will drink of the wine of God's fury, which has been poured full strength into the cup of his wrath. He will be tormented with burning Sulphur in the presence of the holy angels and of the Lamb. And the smoke of their torment rises for ever and ever. There is no rest day or night for those who worship the beast and his image, or for anyone who receives the mark of his name.' This calls for patient endurance on the part of the saints who obey God's commandments and remain faithful to Jesus.

Then I heard a voice from Heaven say, 'Write: Blessed are the dead who die in the Lord from now on.'

'Yes,' says the Spirit, 'they will rest from their labour, for their deeds will follow them.' (Revelation 14:9-13)

A clear warning of the dire consequences for worshiping the Antichrist and taking his mark, this passage also gives us a hint that Tribulation believers will have a different relationship with the Lord from the one enjoyed by the Church. Like Old Testament believers they will be required to keep God's commandments and remain faithful to Jesus to keep their salvation. It appears that they won't be given eternal security but will be responsible for demonstrating their faithfulness by their actions. The only time their work will be done will be after their death. No 'Sabbath rest' for the Tribulation saints. What an absolutely untenable spot to be in. Worship God and die now. Worship the Antichrist and die forever. The voice from Heaven agrees by pronouncing the 2nd of seven blessings in the Revelation. The first was for those who read, hear and take to heart what is written in this book (Revelation 1:3). This one is for those who are martyred for their faith during the Great Tribulation.

The Harvest of the Earth

I looked, and there before me was a white cloud, and seated on the cloud was one 'like a son of man' with a crown of gold on his head and a sharp sickle in his hand. Then another angel came out of the temple and called in a loud voice to him who was sitting on the cloud, 'Take your sickle and reap, because the time to reap has come, for the harvest of the Earth is ripe.' So he who was seated on the cloud swung his sickle over the Earth, and the Earth was harvested. (Revelation 14:14-16)

Some want to see this angel as Jesus, because of the phrase 'son of man.' To me the biggest argument against this is the fact that he's wearing a Stephanos, or victor's crown like the Church wears. Jesus wears a diadem or crown of royalty. But whether he is or is not, the Lord does not affect our understanding of the passage. He's being told to begin the final phase of Earth's judgment.

'Another angel came out of the temple in Heaven, and he too had a sharp sickle. Still another angel, who had charge of the fire, came from the altar and called in a loud voice to him who had the sharp sickle, 'Take your sharp sickle and gather the clusters of grapes from the Earth's vine, because its grapes are ripe.' The angel swung his sickle on the Earth, gathered its grapes and threw them into the great winepress of God's wrath. They were trampled in the winepress outside the city, and blood flowed out of the press, rising as high as the horses' bridles for a distance of 1,600 stadia (Revelation 14:17-20).

This passage, like the one before it, is an overview, a description of things to come. Those being harvested are the non-believers of Earth. We know this because reference is made to the Earth's vine, not the true vine. Also the wine press of God's wrath which is located outside the city symbolizes the coming bowl judgments, culminating in the Battle of Armageddon.

This period of time is also in view in the Kingdom Parable of the Wheat and the Tares, where before the Wheat (sons of the Kingdom) are brought into the Millennium, the sons of the Evil one are harvested and thrown into the fiery furnace. (Matthew 13:36-45) Sons of the Kingdom refers to believers alive on Earth during the Great Tribulation. This shows the extent to which Satan will sacrifice mankind to maintain his hold on Planet Earth. Isaiah 63:1-6 gives us a prophetic view of this time from the Old Testament. It's a conversation between Isaiah and the Lord.

Isaiah: *'Who is this coming from Edom, from Bozrah, with his garments stained crimson? Who is this, robed in splendour, striding forward in the greatness of his strength?'*

The Lord: *'It is I, speaking in righteousness, mighty to save.'*

Isaiah: *'Why are your garments red, like those of one treading the winepress?'*

The Lord: *'I have trodden the winepress alone; from the nations no one was with me. I trampled them in my anger and trod them down in my wrath; their blood spattered my garments, and I stained all my clothing. For the day of vengeance was in my heart, and the year of my redemption has come. I looked, but there was no one to help, I was appalled that no one gave support, so my own arm worked salvation for me, and my own wrath sustained me. I trampled the nations in my anger; in my wrath I made them drunk and poured their blood on the ground.'*

Things are happening pretty fast now, so John has to keep skipping back and forth between things in Heaven and things on Earth, first presenting overviews and then coming back to fill in the details, to make sure we get it all. The main thought here is to convey the extent of the carnage. The average horse's bridle is 4.5 feet off the ground, and 1600 stadia equal about 175 miles. Imagine a river of blood 4.5 feet deep and 175 miles long and you get the idea. If you could drive along its length at 30 miles per hour, it would take nearly 6 hours to cover it all.

'Simplified Summary'

The first half of the seven years, prior to the Lord returning at the end of the Great Tribulation (the last 3½ years) will see the Antichrist solving many problems on Earth and reducing the profound fear of the Ezekiel 38 event and the Rapture. His popularity and amazing knowledge will propel him to stratospheric heights of diplomacy. He will bring the first and only genuine peace treaty together with

Israel and her antagonists and many nations will offer him military and economic support. I believe these will be the Shanghai Treaty Organization's countries and not western powers, many of whom would be weak militarily after the Rapture. The Jews will be very happy with being able to start temple worship again and the government of the day will enter into a 'contract of death' with him. However, many people, both Gentile and Jew alike will know, from hearing the 144 000 witnesses talk or from their own fraternization with the gospel of Jesus Christ, before the Rapture, that this man is full of deceit and lies and that he is not to be trusted. Indeed this is confirmed when his henchman comes along and forces people to worship the Antichrist. Believers in Israel flee 'to the mountains' (Petra) to be supernaturally protected and nourished by Michael the Arch Angel. Daniel 11:41; Revelation 12: 14 and Isaiah 63: 1. Maybe this is when Manna will be used again? Gentile believers go through hell on Earth; cut out of the financial system by the Mark of the Beast and chased whither they may hide. Maybe hiding rifles and loads of ammunition is not so far fetched after all).

Chapter 7

The book of Revelation simplified

If you have had trouble understanding the Book of Revelation, this summary and paraphrase is sure to help. Written as John might have told it today, the Revelation story makes one of the most complex and controversial books of prophecy in the Bible so much easier to comprehend. Faithful to the literal interpretation with just enough background to make it a truly informative, even enjoyable, read.

Chapter 1

I John (who wrote Revelation) was living in exile on the Greek Isle of Patmos when He approached me to undertake the project. Today Patmos is a tourist stop on the sea route from Western Turkey to Athens. It's visited daily by cruise ships and ferry boats crammed with visitors there to get a look at the huge monastery and over 300 little chapels all named after me. But in my time it was a Roman penal colony, a couple of square miles of rock and despair, bleak and lonely. I was there because I would not (could not) stop preaching the Gospel. The authorities had tried all kinds of ways to shut me up but none of them worked so they finally shipped me off to Patmos where I couldn't speak to anybody, or so they thought.

I heard His voice before I saw Him, and when I turned around I fell face down at His feet, knowing it was the Lord. Talk about being scared. Before, He had been more like one of the guys, but now He was King of the Universe. By the way He introduced Himself (as if He needed to) I knew that this was no casual drop-in but an official visit. Something big was in the works.

Although it had been over 50 years since I'd last seen Him, he wasted no time in chit-chat, but immediately instructed me to write a three part letter, a book actually, and send it off to the seven churches He named for me. The three parts were:

❧ things that had been (His time on Earth before the Church was born),
❧ the things that currently were (the church age as represented by the seven congregations He named), and,
❧ the things that would happen after the church age (the Great

Tribulation, His second Coming, and His one thousand year Kingdom.)

Chapter 2-3
He then launched straight into a monologue on these seven churches. It was soon obvious that He had chosen them carefully because by their nature, and in the order He placed them, they chronicled what's now become the history of the church. It would start off small and faithful but would soon grow into a formal organization in danger of forgetting its original purpose, worshiping Him (Ephesus). Its growth would frighten the world governments who would try to suppress it to no avail (Smyrna). Failing in that, they would embrace it and change it from within into a large and powerful government in and of itself, more attuned to the world's ways than His (Pergamus). Near the end of its time the church would split into four components; Catholic (Thyatira), Protestant (Sardis), Evangelical (Philadelphia), and Liberal / New Age (Laodicea). These four would exist side by side until the Rapture, when He would remove those faithful to Him from among all of them, bringing the Church Age to a close and leaving the rest to endure the end time judgments.

Chapter 4
And then something happened that literally blew me away. I looked up and saw this door in the sky standing open and I heard His voice again, commanding me to 'Come up here!' At once I was flung through space and time, landing in a flash before the Throne of God at the end of the Age. There's no way to describe how that felt, one minute standing outside my cave in the 1st century and an instant later standing in Heaven in the 21st, but apparently I was participating in the Rapture of the Church, just like He had promised to the Church at Philadelphia. There were millions of us there; singing praises to God along with all the host of Heaven. We received the crowns we had earned while on Earth and immediately gave them back to Him Who had empowered us to do the things for which we were being rewarded.

Chapter 5
I looked at the Throne of the Almighty and saw Him sitting there holding a document that was no less than the title deed to Planet Earth. It was sealed with seven seals. I sobbed convulsively as I felt the pain God feels at seeing His Creation in terrible bondage, and realizing that no mere human nor even the entire angelic host could free it. But then I saw my Lord Jesus again, still

bearing the awful scars of His crucifixion, and knew that He alone could free the Earth and restore God's creation to Him. By His sacrificial death He had paid its ransom along with yours and mine.

When He took the title deed from His Father, we all recognized that the time had come at last to begin the series of judgments that would rid the world of evil, restore the creation to its Creator and usher in His thousand year reign of peace on Earth. We cheered and shouted and sang till the very heavens shook.

But the one who had stolen the creation was not about to let go without a fight, and incredibly he had enlisted the support of some pretty powerful forces, both natural and supernatural. The biggest, nastiest war in history was spinning up and I had been given the seemingly impossible job of writing the eyewitness account.

I don't know if you can appreciate just how big this job was. I'm nobody's fool, but I was a 1st Century man with a 1st Century vocabulary and I was going to be describing things that were unheard of even at the beginning of the 20th Century. What's more, all the millions of people who would read this account between the time I wrote it and the time the events actually took place would have to be able to understand it. Fortunately I had some supernatural help of my own. First, The Holy Spirit led me to write some of this account as if in a vision rich in symbolism. And second, of the 404 verses in my book, 278 of them are pretty much direct quotes from the Old Testament to help my readers keep things in their proper context and explain the symbolism. (Of course this presumes that you know your Old Testament.)

Chapter 6

Now as I said, the title deed to planet Earth was sealed with seven seals and as the Lord opened them the Holy Spirit gave me visions of judgments being released on Earth. The first four seals were symbolized by horses and riders. In the first one a white horse appeared ridden by someone coming as a conqueror bent on conquest. He's trying to look like Christ but close inspection reveals that he's an impostor, the Antichrist. For one thing he's wearing the wrong crown. It's a victor's crown not one for a king. Since he had a bow but no arrows, he was not ready for war yet but that would soon change.

The second horse was fiery red and symbolized war. It was followed, as so often happens after wars begin, by a black horse symbolizing famine. Most people would now have to work all day just to buy a loaf of bread, but the rich would not be affected yet.

The fourth horse was a sickly green colour and symbolized the death that follows war and famine. In fact more than 1/4th of the worlds population (that's over 1.5 billion people) will die in this series of judgments.

When He broke open the 5th seal, I saw all those who had been martyred for their faith. They cried out to God for vengeance, but He told them to be patient because still more would die and join them. Seeing all the people who had been and would be slaughtered simply for believing in their Creator must have angered God because as the 6th seal was broken He unleashed a colossal earthquake on the Earth. Smoke and dust rose into the sky until the sun and moon were blotted out. The mountains and islands shook from the power of the quake, and all mankind fled for cover, hiding in caves and among rocks, knowing that the wrath of God was behind this.

Chapter 7

Because even in wrath God remembers mercy, He paused then to commission 144,000 Jews, 12,000 from each of the 12 tribes of Israel to go out among the people of the Earth and once again spread the Gospel into every nation and in every language. And just then all those who had not become believers until after the Rapture, but had died in faith during this series of judgments arrived in Heaven all dressed in white and waving palm branches. They stood before the Throne of God and praised Him saying, 'Salvation belongs to our God and to the Lamb!' Immediately all the Heavenly host joined them in worshiping God. These Tribulation Saints were assigned the special honour of serving God in His Temple, never again to hunger or thirst or feel any discomfort, for the Lamb of God had become their Shepherd.

The first series of judgments caused astounding devastation on Earth, but it also brought many millions of new believers into an everlasting union with their Creator. Before this seven-year period is over more people will come to faith than in all the History of Man preceding. But it's also the time when the full extent of unregenerate man's depravity is made clear. The middle ground will completely disappear as the People of Earth face their most perilous times ever.

Chapter 8

When the Lord broke open the 7th and final seal of the title deed to planet Earth, there was silence in Heaven for about half an hour. The first 6 had caused so much havoc on Earth that I will bet almost everyone in Heaven was literally holding his breath to see what the 7th seal would bring. I know I was.

I looked up and saw seven angels standing before God. Each was given a long trumpet, the kind a herald would use on Earth to announce the arrival of an important dignitary or event. And another angel appeared with a golden censor filled with incense representing the prayers of all the saints that he placed on the golden altar before the Throne. As the smoke from the incense rose up before God, the angel used the censer to scoop up the fire from the altar and hurl it down upon the Earth. Immediately there was thunder, lightning, and another earthquake. More judgments were coming, worse than the ones just past. When the first angel blew his trumpet a storm of hail and fire mixed with blood arose on Earth burning up 1/3 of the Earth's trees and vegetation. As the second angel blew his trumpet, a giant meteor the size of a mountain came crashing into the Earth, landing in the ocean. The force of the impact turned the ocean red like blood and killed 1/3 of all the creatures living in it. Over 16 thousand ships were destroyed and 500 thousand sailors killed from the storms and tidal waves caused by the meteor's impact. At the sound of the 3rd trumpet, another blazing star, called Wormwood, fell from the sky contaminating 1/3 of the Earth's fresh water supply, and causing many more deaths. As the 4th trumpet sounded the devastation from the hail storm and the two meteor impacts caused smoke and dust to rise into the atmosphere reducing the light from the sun, moon and stars by 1/3 and causing periods of total blackness both day and night.

As if things on Earth weren't bad enough, I heard the voice of an angel warning people to prepare for even worse disasters when the remaining 3 trumpets were sounded. Something much more frightening was clearly in store.

Chapter 9

As the 5th angel sounded his trumpet I got a glimpse of our great enemy. Back when I was one of the Lords first disciples, He had mentioned seeing Satan fall like a star from Heaven (Luke 10:18), and now Satan was being given the key to the Abyss, or underworld. As he unlocked it, smoke rose up as if from a gigantic furnace, and out of the smoke appeared swarms of hideous insects that at first looked to me like locusts. But as I observed them more closely, I decided that they had to be some sort of demonic manifestation. Real locusts are vegetarian, but these things were not allowed to harm any vegetation, nor could they attack the people of God still on Earth. But they could sting those people who were not supernaturally protected and when they did the pain was incredible. The sting from these locust things was not fatal but it left their victims in unbearable pain for five months. Believe me, they all wished they were dead.

Here's where my first century experience was unequal to the task. These locusts looked like nothing I had ever seen, and in all the centuries since I wrote this account, nothing like them has ever been seen on Earth by anyone else either. Maybe they're some sort of weapons system born out of 21st Century technology or maybe they are some invention of the Devil. One thing is certain; they're straight out of the pits of hell. The one who unlocked the Abyss controlled them. He called himself 'The Destroyer.' Amazing grasp of the obvious, that one!

When the 6th trumpet was blown, an invisible barrier came down on Earth. The Euphrates River has always been the traditional boundary between East and West. It starts in the Mountains of Turkey and flows southward through Syria and Iraq emptying into the Persian Gulf. Culture, language, custom and religion all change dramatically when you cross the Euphrates, and for centuries it's width and depth prevented the armies of both eastern and western nations from crossing. But now this barrier, represented by four bound angels, was being lowered and a massive army, *two hundred million* strong, was on the march. Before this army was finished, fully a third of the world's remaining population would die. These deaths, when added to the ones from the earlier judgments would bring the total dead to over three billion, about half the Earth's population. Once again my experience was inadequate to the task of describing the appearance and weaponry of this huge army, but suffice it to say that it was a fearsome and awful sight to behold.

You'd think with those demonic locusts attacking only non-believers and three billion people being killed from wars and other disasters, that people would be flocking to the Lord in search of comfort and security. But this just didn't happen, and I'll tell you why.

There is a belief floating around that's as old as mankind but in the last days will become a religion that deceives almost everybody. It's called the

Luciferian Doctrine and understanding it helps explain why the world won't turn to its Creator in this, the worst time in human history. The Luciferian doctrine is named of course after Lucifer, a Latin name that translates 'light bearer', and holds that Lucifer is the good guy trying to enlighten the people of the world in preparation for the spiritual evolution necessary to bring peace to all mankind. According to Luciferian Doctrine our physical evolution is finished and all we need to do now is throw off the bonds of Judeo-Christian thinking to complete our spiritual evolution and enter into the Utopian Era. But Lucifer's being hindered in all this by the evil Adonai (Hebrew for Lord) Who, along with His followers, is working to thwart Lucifer's grand plan by requiring everyone to adhere to His reactionary religion, effectively preventing our spiritual evolution. In order for humanity to achieve Utopia those who insist on clinging to their obsolete Judeo- Christian faith have to be eliminated. The Great Tribulation is characterized in Luciferian Doctrine as the evil Adonai's last great effort to destroy mankind's 'light bearer' and prevent our ascension into Utopia, keeping us in bondage to Him.

Following the Church's disappearance the Truth became pretty scarce on Earth and the whole world was deceived into believing the Luciferian Doctrine just as my friend Paul warned would happen (2 Thessalonians 2:9-12). So naturally, thinking the Lord is the bad guy, they became even more intense in their worship of Lucifer, hoping that he would prevail and bring an end to their suffering. (There is a way that seems right to man, but the end thereof is death … Proverbs 14:12) Lucifer, of course, is also widely known as Satan or The Devil.

Chapter 10

Like He did after opening the 6th seal, the Lord paused now after the 6th trumpet had sounded to provide some insight on what was about to happen. A huge and mighty angel appeared as if in a vision and planted his right foot on the sea and his left one on the land. This symbolized the fact that what was coming would affect the destinies of all living things on Earth, whether on land or in the sea, and all peoples. As he raised his voice to the heavens, I heard seven peals of thunder, each one a description of judgments to come. Before I could write down what I had heard, the Lord commanded me not to do it. The information contained in these 7 peals of thunder was to remain secret until the appointed time.

Then the giant angel shouted, 'There will be no more delay!' When the

7th angel begins to sound his trumpet all the end-time prophecies will finally come to pass. Then the Lord told me to take the scroll that the giant angel was holding, and as I did he commanded me to eat it. At first taste, it seemed sweet as honey, but after I swallowed it, my stomach turned sour. This is to signify that the fulfilment of prophecy, when the Lord rights all the wrongs done through the ages to Him and His people, takes back all that has been stolen from Him, and puts His enemies to utter defeat, is anticipated with much excitement and joy by His people. But the horror and carnage of the warfare required to accomplish this is enough to make you sick.

In addition to the problems caused by my limited language and experience, I soon realized I had another even bigger challenge in writing this story. Even though events on Earth and events in Heaven were sometimes happening all at once, I could only write about them one at a time. Its kind of like the football commentator trying to describe the actions of all the twenty two players on the field in a play that lasted only about thirty seconds. It takes longer to tell about it than it did to do it, so he has to 'stop the play' from time to time to explain certain parts of it.

With the vision of the giant angel we had entered into a time where lots of things are happening all at once, some on Earth and some in Heaven. Like the football commentator, I'll have to 'stop the play' a couple of times in order to describe what I saw. (This is why the book of Revelation appears to be out of chronological order in some places).

Chapter 11

As the end of the age was drawing near, the Lord had made Himself known to the People of Israel again just as Ezekiel had foretold two thousand five hundred years earlier, and in response they had built a temple for worshiping Him again like they did in Old Testament days. I was told to go and measure the temple area but to leave out the outer court because it had been defiled by a non-Jewish element whose real intent was to pay homage to a false messiah. These Gentiles were forcing their way into the Lord's Holy City and would desecrate it for 42 months with their false worship. The Luciferian Doctrine I told you about last time was becoming the dominant religion of the world and the 3 1/2; year long Great Tribulation would soon be upon them.

To warn them against this false religion, the Lord sent two witnesses to preach the true gospel in Israel. To help His people identify these two and lend credibility to their warnings, He gave them the same supernatural powers they had displayed during their lifetimes in the Old Testament. Like Elijah, one had the power to prevent any rain from falling on Earth, and like Moses the other one could turn water into blood and strike the Earth with all kinds of plagues. Of course, the leaders of the 'new' religion tried to have them silenced, but the Lord protected them all through their 1260-day ministry. When their assignment was finished He allowed them to be killed, and to show their contempt, the people left them lying where they had fallen in the streets of Jerusalem and sent gifts to each other to celebrate finally being rid of their tormenting. But after 3 1/2; days they heard the same loud command I'd been given earlier. 'Come up here!' the Lord shouted, and in full view of all the world these two dead bodies stood up and shot up into Heaven, full of life. At that moment there was another earthquake, part of Jerusalem was destroyed and thousands were killed. The survivors were terrified and correctly identified God as the source of the quake. He always has the last word, does he not!

Just then the 7th trumpet sounded and loud voices in Heaven announced, 'The Kingdoms of the world have become the Kingdom of our Lord and of His Messiah, and He will reign for ever and ever!' As the twenty four leaders of the church whose thrones surrounded the Throne of God worshiped and sang praises to Him, I couldn't help but think about that scroll I had eaten. Hearing that the time had finally come to begin the Lord's reign on Earth caused my heart to swell with joy, but knowing that the full fury of God's wrath was about to be unleashed on His enemies also filled me with a sense of dread.

Then God's real Temple, the one in Heaven, was opened and I saw the Ark of the Covenant, symbol of His commandments and promises to His people. The flashes of lightning, peals of thunder, earthquake and hailstorm that came next warned of the final and most terrifying series of judgments soon to descend upon the Earth.

Chapter 12

Now comes one of those times I talked about when we will have to 'stop the play' so to speak.

To give me a better perspective and show just who was the cause of all this horror and devastation, the Lord gave me a quick history lesson in the form of another vision. First I saw a woman, representing the human race in general but Israel in particular. She was about to give birth to the Messiah.

Then I saw this enormous red dragon with extraordinary intellect, power, and authority. He had rebelled against God and convinced one third of the angelic host to follow him. He stood waiting to destroy the Messiah the moment He was born. But God raised His Messiah from the dead and whisked Him up to Heaven. The woman fled into the desert to a place God had prepared for her to hide from the dragon during the time of his great war against God. This war began in Heaven, but Michael, General of the Lord's army, defeated the dragon and drove him from Heaven confining him and his forces to Earth.

Then I learned that the dragon is the Devil, or Satan. Ever since he deceived Adam and Eve and illegally gained control of Earth he's been at war with God to keep it. He's also been trying to win the people of Earth over to his side by deceiving them just like he did with Adam and Eve and the angels. He knew the Messiah was coming to take back the Earth and redeem God's people and that's why he killed Him. But when God raised His Messiah from the dead He promised to send Him back to finish the job. Since the Messiah first came to Earth through the Jewish people, Satan has been determined destroy them all, to prevent them from calling Him back again. This is what makes anti-Semitism the most brutal of all bigotry. It's Satanic.

When Satan realized he had been confined to Earth he unleashed his full fury against God's people. Foreseeing this God had done two things. First, as a reward for their faith, He had snatched His Church right off the Earth altogether and hidden them some years earlier in a place he had prepared for them in Heaven. And second He had hidden the believing remnant of Israel in the desert on Earth, east of the Dead Sea.

Chapter 13

For his part, Satan empowered two men to deceive the people of Earth and mobilize them against God and His people. These men were identified to me in the vision as two beasts, one from the sea and one from the land. The first was a great political leader, the smartest, most charismatic man the world has ever known. When this man was apparently assassinated Satan supernaturally healed him, convincing the world he was the messiah. Nearly everyone on Earth was fooled by this so-called resurrection and began worshiping Satan and his false messiah. Remember I told you that after the Church disappeared, God's Word was pretty scarce on Earth and non-believers were easily tricked by what they saw. Also, having previously hardened their hearts against the truth they were now fair game for the lie. I have to admit, it was pretty convincing. If I hadn't had the benefit of the Holy Spirit dwelling within me I'd have been fooled, too.

Satan's second man was a religious leader. His job was to head up the world's new religion and make sure everyone worshiped Satan and his false messiah. Using the supernatural powers Satan had given him, he performed all sorts of miraculous signs even constructing a giant image of the false messiah that could actually speak. To ensure their loyalty to his religion and compliance with its ritual, he fixed it so that people could not earn money or buy the things they needed unless they took a mark signifying their belief in the false messiah. Refusing to receive the mark was punishable by death. From now on, following Jesus was going to require a whole bunch of faith.

With the appearance of these two men, all hell had broken loose on Earth and the Great Tribulation had begun. Because of this vision I now understood that Satan was the cause of all of man's troubles. With his successful effort in deceiving Adam and Eve he had introduced sin and sickness and death and destruction into God's perfect creation contaminating it beyond repair and estranging God from man. In His great mercy, God had provided mankind a remedy for this predicament and through His prophets had pleaded with us to accept it, even sending His own Son to show us the way.

But even God runs out of patience and now the time had come to take back that which had been stolen from Him and punish those responsible. Satan and his angels (demons) along with all those from the human race who sided with him would now learn the terrible consequences that come from incurring the wrath of the Living God and refusing His offer of peace. But even in the midst of His wrath, God would still accept without prejudice all who bowed their knee to Him and asked forgiveness.

Chapter 14

The Lord gave me the duration of the Great Tribulation in several ways. They come out equal when you realize He's measuring time the way He created it; twelve thirty-day months for a 360 day year. So whether He says 3 1/2; years or 42 months or 1260 days it's all the same. With Satan's expulsion from Heaven and the appearance of Antichrist as a self proclaimed god on Earth the last 3 1/2; years of the Age of Man have begun. This is the Great Tribulation.

I had been trying to absorb the vision of the woman, the red dragon and the two beasts when my attention was drawn back to Heaven. There I saw another group numbering 144,000 but different than the 12,000 Jews from each of the 12 tribes of Israel I described earlier. That group was composed of Jewish believers commissioned to spread the Gospel on Earth. These were standing before God's throne in Heaven, having been redeemed from the Earth. Since they are described as pure and blameless, purchased from among men and offered as firstfruits to God who follow the Lamb wherever He goes, they can only represent the Raptured Church, observing events of the Great Tribulation from their vantage point in Heaven. No group of humans could ever be described that way unless the Lord had first perfected them as happens in the Rapture.

By the way, when I say they had not defiled themselves with women, I don't mean there's anything wrong with women per se. But most of natural man's evil thoughts involve sinning with women, and in my day the false religions used illicit sexual acts with women in their worship rituals. As an example the great temple of Aphrodite in Corinth was home to nearly 1000 female priests who supported the temple's financial needs by getting sailors and other travellers who visited Corinth from all over the middle east to pay to have sex with them. Sex was all mixed up with pagan religion then just like it's all mixed up with politics now.

As I looked around I also saw three angels flying between Heaven and Earth broadcasting messages. One was proclaiming the eternal gospel to all the nations in every language, and alerting them to the judgments still to come. Another was giving news of the coming destruction of Babylon, that great city that has personified all that's opposed to God on Earth. And the third was warning the people of Earth that worshiping Antichrist and receiving his mark was an irreversible decision that would condemn them to never ending pain and torment. I told you the middle ground was disappearing. Worship the Lord and face the death penalty on Earth or worship Satan and face eternal punishment in Hell. Talk about needing faith.

Then the Lord showed me another vision. In this one a harvest of grapes from all over the Earth was brought to Israel to be crushed in the winepress of God's Wrath creating a great river of blood. It was up to four and a half feet deep and one hundred and seventy five miles long, the distance from Mt. Megiddo in central Israel to the Dead Sea in the south. This was a vision of the soon coming Battle of Armageddon, the great and final thrust in Satan's war for control of Earth. (Since the Hebrew word for Mount is Har, over the centuries what was Har Megiddo in Hebrew has become Armageddon in English.)

Chapter 15

Back in Heaven seven angels appeared along with the seven golden bowls of God's Wrath, His last series of judgments. When these were over His enemies would be vanquished and His victory complete. Just then another large group of martyrs arrived from Earth and stood before His throne. They were some of the last believers left and had been executed for their refusal to take the mark. Now they stood in Heaven singing praises to God: their faith had been justified. I was reminded of that verse in Isaiah about the righteous perishing to be spared from evil (Isaiah. 57:1).

The doors to Heaven's Temple opened and the seven angels were handed the seven golden bowls. As they went forth the doors were shut so that no one could enter signifying that nothing could interfere with the dispensing of these final judgments. God takes no pleasure from judging even His enemies and remained inside the Temple to suffer in anguish alone.

Chapter 16

As the first bowl was poured out upon the Earth ugly and painful sores broke out on those who had taken the mark and worshiped the Antichrist. Their torment had begun. The second bowl turned all the seas to blood and every living creature remaining in them died. The third bowl contaminated all the world's fresh water supply, turning it to blood as well. In doing this, God was avenging the blood of all His martyrs slain throughout the Age of Man from the prophets of old right through to the very last ones newly arrived in Heaven, by giving His enemies blood to drink.

The fourth bowl judgment increased the heat from the Sun to a point where people actually caught fire from direct exposure to its rays. Incredibly they cursed God's name, having become so confused by the Luciferian Doctrine that they thought He was their enemy.

With the fifth bowl, everything went pitch black. The light from the Sun and Moon went out, electricity refused to work, and even fires would not give off any light. This scared people so much they could hardly stand it, but still they cursed God and refused His offer of peace.

With the sixth bowl the River Euphrates went dry, removing for good the natural boundary between East and West that had begun to come down with the sixth trumpet. The armies of the Eastern Nations saw their chance to steal across and join the battle for control of Planet Earth. Demonic spirits from the unholy trinity of Satan, the Antichrist and the False Prophet went through out the world performing miraculous signs and enticing the leaders of all the world's armies to come and join the fray. Before they were finished close to 400 million soldiers would show up in the Middle East, armed to the teeth and spoiling for a fight. This would really be 'the mother of all battles.' I realized that my vision of a 175 mile river of blood was no exaggeration.

When the seventh angel poured out his bowl, I heard the voice of God saying, 'It is done!' The thunder and lightning, and the greatest earthquake in history told me the judgments were going out in full force.

But this time something unique was added. The Old Testament punishment for blasphemy was death by stoning. The people of Earth had cursed and blasphemed the name of God to no end, and now they were receiving the penalty for their crimes. Giant hailstones weighing upwards of 100 pounds each fell upon the Earth and men scattered like ants, cursing Him as they ran for cover.

Chapter 17

As all this was happening, one of the seven angels came over to explain why these judgments were necessary. In a vision He showed me a woman sitting atop a scarlet beast that had seven heads and ten horns. They were riding across many waters. This woman (he called her mystery Babylon) represents the false religions that have deceived and persecuted God's people, and the beast represents Satan. The angel wanted me to understand that Satan has always used false religion to steal people away from God. Not many have ever been seduced directly into devil worship, so he has used the worship of anything other than God, especially those things that seem good or enjoyable, to deceive mankind and lead them unknowingly to their destruction. He has also used the followers of these false religions to persecute believers who refuse to join them, or who insist on spreading the True Gospel.

The seven heads stand for seven world powers that have challenged God's authority over His creation through the age of man. All these world powers were built by Satan to glorify his false religions and alienate people from their Creator. At the time I was writing this five had already come and gone; Egypt, Assyria, Babylon, Persia, and Greece. The one currently in power was Rome, and the one to come at the end would be a revival of the Roman Empire with elements of Babylon, Persia and Greece mixed in to spice things up. The Antichrist will emerge from this last group.

The ten horns stand for ten leaders the Antichrist will appoint to help administer his power at the end of the age. They'll be loyal to the Antichrist, supporting his efforts to overpower the Lord. But the Lord will prevail, and when He comes to defeat them, He will bring His church back from Heaven with Him.

The many waters stand for all the people of the world deceived by Satan's false religions. When he comes to power, the Antichrist will abolish all these false religions since they were just the means to an end and proclaim himself to be god. Because of the successful promotion of the Luciferian Doctrine, and since almost all of the remaining believers will have been martyred for their faith, most people will accept this and knowingly become Satan worshipers (which has really been his goal from the very beginning). God will let this happen to pierce the veil of deception woven by false religion, and let people see who they have really been worshiping all along.

Because of God's patience, not wanting any to perish but all to come to repentance, He has restrained Himself all through the age. During this time His enemies, mistaking kindness for weakness, have gone way over the line and so His judgment, when it comes, has to fit the magnitude of the crime. Billions have been deceived and lost and those responsible must pay the consequences. So that's why this final round of judgments has to be so severe.

Chapter 18

The last bastion of Satan's deceptive practices will be found in the City of Babylon. In the end times this city on the banks of the Euphrates in modern Iraq will become the world's centre for the three major elements of society; religion, commerce, and government. Man's religion which has imprisoned people spiritually, man's commerce which has imprisoned them economically, and man's government which has imprisoned them socially must all be defeated to bring the freedoms promised in God's Kingdom. At the end of the age Babylon is the centre and the symbol of all that's wrong with man's way and it has to be destroyed forever. And when it is the people of Earth will stand in shock at how quickly it fell. O Babylon, city of power! In one hour your doom has come. With the defeat of Babylon, God's enemies have finally been made a footstool under His Feet, and the way is now clear for the Lord to return as the conquering King to establish his Kingdom. The magnitude of the shouting and singing in Heaven rocked the universe. Hallelujah!

Chapter 19

With the final and total destruction of Babylon, God's enemies have been all but defeated and the war for Planet Earth is just about over. 'Hallelujah,' we all shouted from Heaven, 'For our Lord God Almighty reigns!' Hallelujah is a Hebrew word meaning 'Praise the Lord' and after the fact I was surprised to learn that I'm the only New Testament writer who used it. I guess the Lord was saving it for just this occasion. It certainly applies.

I looked around again and saw Heaven standing open and there before me was a rider on a white horse. Unlike the one I had seen in a vision at the beginning of my story, this one was the real thing. He was even wearing the right crown, the crown of royalty. So there would be no mistaking His identity, I gave Him the name I had coined in my gospel account; the Word of God. The armies of Heaven were with Him on white horses of their own, all clean and dressed in white linen. By the blood on His garments and the absence of any on theirs it was clear that He was defeating His enemies all by Himself, just as Isaiah had foretold. (Isaiah. 63:1-6) No babe in arms this time, He's here to assume command of His creation and won't be taking any guff from anyone.

Down on Earth the Antichrist and the armies of all the nations gathered together for their final stand, but just like that He wiped them all out. As opposed to the bow without arrows carried by the impostor in my earlier vision, the Lord spoke with such power and authority it's as if His words were a sharp double edged sword. He is the King of Kings and Lord of Lords! The Antichrist and false prophet were captured alive, but all it took for all the armies of Earth to be slain in their tracks was the sound of His voice. God summoned demonic creatures that looked like birds to consume their dead flesh. The Antichrist and false prophet were thrown alive into the place of eternal suffering reserved for Satan and his followers, to be tormented forever.

Chapter 20

And then the most incredible thing happened. An angel with a great chain and the key to the underworld came down from Heaven. He single-handedly captured Satan, bound him with the chain and locked him away for a thousand years. Satan has one more appearance to make in God's Grand Design but for the duration of the Millennium he will be in solitary confinement.

Then all those who refused to worship the Antichrist and had been martyred for their faith in the Lord were brought back to life to reign with

Christ for one thousand years. With this event, the first resurrection that had begun with Jesus Himself coming out of the grave, was over. All those who died in faith from the cross till now, together with those Raptured with the Church, were alive again to receive the blessings of the Kingdom Age.

This is a good time to remind you that the Bible, being God's Word for the age of man, does not speak of events that take place before the Creation or after the Millennium. But so you will know his ultimate disposition, at the very end of our Lord's one thousand year reign on Earth, Satan is set free again. And without a speck of remorse or any evidence of a change of heart, he immediately begins recruiting a massive army to go up against God one more time. And can you believe it, even after one thousand years of peace under the perfect rule of the Lord Himself, and with the lessons of history to teach them what happened the last time someone took on the Lord, a huge mass of people responds to his call. But the Lord sends down fire from Heaven and devours them all in a flash. Then that old devil Satan is thrown into the place of eternal suffering to join the Antichrist and the false prophet to be tormented day and night for ever and ever. And with that we are finally rid of him.

I have often wondered why the Lord placed this one thousand year period between time and eternity. I guess I have come to the conclusion that it's to shatter all our excuses for our behaviour. Ever since the Garden of Eden, we have been blaming outside circumstances each time we're caught sinning. First we say, 'The devil made me do it'. So in the Millennium God has Satan chained and imprisoned. Then we say, 'If only you hadn't gone away and left us.' So He comes back to personally rule over us. Then we say, 'It's the bad example of all those unbelievers.' So He takes all the unbelievers off the planet at the beginning of the Millennium and leaves only those who have survived the Great Tribulation and professed their faith in Him to repopulate the Earth. (Note: See Matthew. 25:31-46). And after one thousand years of Heaven on Earth, there's still enough sin in the hearts of unregenerate man to staff Satan's final rebellion the minute he's freed. Even under ideal conditions such as these, natural man cannot behave well enough to please God and will rebel against His authority the first chance he gets. Only after he's perfected by God can man hope to please Him. Our need for a Saviour is indisputable.

One more thing happens at the very end of the Millennium. After Satan's been dealt with, the Lord brings all the unsaved dead back to life for their final judgment. Boy are they surprised! Having lived their lives ignoring or denying God, they now stand face to face with Him to explain their behaviour. As the events of their lives are reviewed, all the times they heard and rejected the gospel are pointed out. And having refused God's offer of pardon, they now become accountable for their sins. They're judged and thrown into the place of eternal suffering. It's such a shame. The place was created for Satan and his angels so man has to choose to go there. He does so by committing the one unpardonable sin, refusing God's remedy in favour of his own.

Chapter 21

With those two glimpses of the end of the Millennium, let's go back to its beginning. Before my very eyes, I saw Heaven and Earth restored to their original condition before sin entered the world and messed things up. I realized that some of the 'natural disasters' that took place during the Tribulation were actually re-shaping the Earth and changing its orbit to permit this restoration.

Then I saw the New Jerusalem coming down out of the sky to enter its orbit near Earth. Because of its size, which I will detail in a minute, and the fact that only perfected believers can live there, there's no way this city could ever be a part of Earth, but it has to be near to permit travel back and forth. The city was absolutely huge, over 1400 miles square and 1400 miles high. Some speculate that there's enough room there for each and every believer to have his own 182,000 square foot mansion. The city had 12 gates, one each for the 12 tribes of Israel and each made of a single pearl. (That's a hoot! Oysters aren't even kosher.) It also had 12 foundations covered with precious gems, named for the 12 apostles. There was not any temple in the city, nor did it need the light from the sun or moon because the Father and the Son both dwell there. Their Presence provides all the light that's necessary. Leaders of all the nations of Earth come and pay tribute bringing all their honour and glory, but no one impure can ever enter, only those whose names are written in the Lamb's Book of Life.

Chapter 22

On Earth a Great Temple, built in Israel to glorify God, gushed forth a giant spring of fresh pure water. It became a river that flowed west to the Mediterranean and east to the Dead Sea. Its waters freshened the Dead Sea and permitted fish to flourish there (see Ezekiel 47). All along the river's banks fruit trees grew, each bearing a new crop every month of the year. Their leaves had healing power, and the fruit was delicious to eat. Near the Temple the Father and Son had their Throne, and from there they would rule the world for ever and ever.

I was so overcome with joy at seeing all the splendour that God has in store for those who love Him that I fell at the feet of the angel who was showing it to me, and he scolded me, exclaiming 'Worship God alone!'. Good advice.

Then my Lord said, 'Behold I am coming soon! My reward is with Me, and I will give to everyone according to what he has done.' I could see that He meant that God in His infinite wisdom has given all of us all the right to choose our own destiny. By what He showed me it's obvious that everyone ever born lives forever. The only question is where we will spend eternity. Choose Him and receive eternal life in the City of God. Reject Him and it's eternal punishment with Satan and his followers in his place of torment. The choice has never been so clear.

He then told me to warn all of the millions who would read this letter down through the centuries. Take this message seriously! Grave consequences would await the one who either adds to or tries to dilute its purpose and content. But as He told me at the beginning, great blessings would come to the ones who read, hear and take to heart what I have written. To this I say, Amen: Come, Lord Jesus. The grace of the Lord Jesus be with God's people. Amen.

❧ ❧

Some other interesting points

1. The Muslim war against the Antichrist

It's my own personal view that the Antichrist will initially use the power base of Islam to rise to power, with supernatural abilities to boot. However, when the Antichrist declares himself to be God, Muslim hordes, known as the Kings of the South (predominantly Sunni) and the Kings of the North (predominantly Shia) will turn on him with great fury, as his claim to deity will be pure blasphemy to them. However his ten nation power base will rescue him and he will continue his blasphemy against the only God.

2. The rescue of the Jewish remnant by the Archangel Michael

When Satan indwells the Antichrist, he becomes furious that people still serve Christ even after the Rapture. He kills many gentile believers, even as the Antichrist did prior to being indwelt by Satan, but he is robbed of killing Jewish believers because they flee to the hills of (many scholars believe) Petra in south Jordan. This is a vast, rugged area that is capable of hiding an entire army.

The Jews that do not turn to Christ, but have rather formed a pact with the Antichrist when they signed his peace treaty with Islam, learn to their horror that Satan, indwelt in the Antichrist, now turns on them in great fury, inviting the world to finally destroy Israel in what will become known as the battle of Armageddon, where Christ Himself slays the armies of the world.

Chapter 8

The Battle of Armageddon
– an overview

To understand what leads up to the battle of Armageddon, we have to wind the clock back about 2300 years to when Alexander the Great conquered land all the way up to India and down to Egypt. When he died in 323 BC he was succeeded by four surviving generals who split up his dynasty. To cut a long and very complicated story short, the biggest area to the north and east was taken by Seleucus and Egypt was taken by Ptolemy. They became known as the Seleucid and Ptolemaic Kingdoms, or the King of the North and the King of the South (as a matter of interest Cleopatra V11 was the last Ptolemaic ruler).

In modern times the Kings of the South have become the Sunni dominant nations of all of north Africa, Jordan, Saudi Arabia and out on a leg, Turkey. The Kings of the North belong to the Shia branch of Islam and are Iran, Iraq (although with a very big Sunni minority) and Syria's minority, but ruling, Alawites who are a sub-sect of Shia Islam. (A later chapter will describe what a huge influence President Obama had on the expansion of the 'Kings of the South' countries and the coming together of the 'Northern Kingdom' in various alliances.)

Fast forward to the beginning of the Great Tribulation, which starts half way through Daniel's 70 weeks prophecy and the Antichrist has claimed himself to be God and must be worshipped by all. You will have noticed by now that all said countries are Islamic, with Shia facing down Sunni wherever possible. However, both Sunni and Shia believe that their end time saviour, or Mhadi, will come with Jesus (sic) to destroy the Antichrist, while the Christian perspective is that the Islamic Mhadi *IS* THE Antichrist!

A man, even a very well respected and admired man with amazing powers that announces to the world that he is God is bound to cause the Islamic leaders of the North (Shia) and South countries (Sunni) to rise up in absolute horror and attack him (Daniel 11: 36- 40 and repeated in 2 Thessalonians 2:4 and Revelation 13:6). The Antichrist will be ruling in Babylon at this time.

It's clear the armies attacking the Antichrist will be enraged Muslims, screaming blasphemy at the top of their lungs but who will defend the Antichrist?

I believe it will be the unredeemed Israeli soldiers plus Russia and China, plus troops from the Shanghai Treaty countries, which would be a vast and incredibly powerful force, much stronger than the West's armies which would have been weakened by the Rapture. They will smash all Islamic forces in front of them as they come through and occupy said countries. Thus the phrase *'Who is like the beast, who can war against him?'* will be realised (Revelation 13:4). This very short, brutal and unforgiving war, with no prisoners taken, will elevate the Antichrist to God-like status.

However, wars will swirl around the world as law and order breaks down and leaders are overthrown. I believe the armies that help the Antichrist are mainly eastern, along with Russia. They will be survivors from a terrible war in the far east that kills over 2 billion people (Revelation 9). The Great Tribulation will be a time so terrifying, with earthquakes and famines and Tsunamis so vast that ships and coastal cities will be flooded, that all mankind would be wiped out lest God put an end to it, which He does at his second coming and the battle of Armageddon.

It is to this 'battle' that we now turn. Firstly, we need to understand that the Ezekiel 38 'war' and Armageddon are not the same wars. Christians who believe so become very confused in their understanding of end time events. The Ezekiel event includes specific, listed countries while Armageddon involves armies from the whole world. Furthermore, the armies in the Ezekiel event are destroyed by acts of God while in the Armageddon event the armies are destroyed by Jesus Himself.

Having defeated the threat from the north and east, which may have been localised countries like Turkey, Saudi Arabia and Iran trying to undo their defeat at the hands of the Antichrist, a totally new situation arises for the him to deal with but we need to go back a step first.

Just prior to Satan indwelling the human body of the Antichrist, a war had taken place in Heaven with Michael the Arch Angel versus Satan (Revelation 12: 7-12). The result of this war is that Satan was booted out of Heaven once and for all and entered the Earthly plane. He was full of wrath for this and the world succumbed to God's Wrath for the next 3 ½ years. One of his first acts after defeating the Kings of the North and South was to get rid of every Jew in Israel and hopefully the whole Earth. He turned on them and attacked them, possibly with Russian and Chinese troops [Author's assumption]. The Jews will put up a sterling fight but will have handed most of their military equipment over to world monitoring forces as part of the major peace treaty so two thirds of the population will be killed. The remaining third will have their eyes opened and know that God is real and turn from their alliance with the Antichrist. They and the Jews that have already accepted Christ will escape to Petra, where Michael the Archangel will protect and nourish them (Zechariah 13: 8-9 and Revelation 12: 14).

The stage is now set for the battle of Armageddon. The Antichrist, with the full Satanic knowledge of Satan himself will know that God will intervene to restore Israel and sends three evil spirits (Revelation 16 : 13-14) into the world to call all nations to come to protect his kingdom Israel from God. Why would the world believe the Antichrist that they could win the battle, you may ask? The answer is simple. The world by this stage is so dark and evil, with people's hearts totally corrupted that they will believe the lie that the Antichrist is God and that the coming forces that want to attack Israel are evil, responsible for all the chaos the world has seen (Revelation 13:4 says : *'Men worshiped the dragon (Satan) because he had given authority to the beast (Antichrist), and they also worshiped the beast and asked, "Who is like the beast? Who can make war against him?"*). People of the world had become so duped into believing the lie that the Antichrist is God that they send many millions of men to the valley of Megiddo in Jezreel, the northern part of Israel (Revelation 16:16). This is where they wait for the real God's forces to attack them, Who turns out to be one Person, Jesus Christ Himself.

Imagine their shock and horror as Christ arrives above them and using the power of His Word (no bombs or missiles or tanks) totally and utterly destroys them. The destruction is so great that the level of blood is as deep as a horse's bridal and spreads over 175 miles in length.

The return of Christ is described Revelation 19: 19 – *'And I saw the beast, the kings of the Earth, and their armies, gathered together to make war against Him who sat on the horse and against His army. (20) Then the beast was captured, and with him the false prophet who worked signs in his presence, by which he deceived those who received the mark of the beast and those who worshiped his image. These two were cast alive into the lake of fire burning with brimstone. (21) And the rest were killed with the sword which proceeded from the mouth of Him who sat on the horse. And all the birds were filled with their flesh'*.

Jesus is described thus in Revelation 19:12 : *'His eyes were like a flame of fire, and on His head were many crowns. He [e]had a name written that no one knew except Himself. (13) He was clothed with a robe dipped in blood, and His name is called The Word of God. (14) And the armies in Heaven, clothed in fine linen, white and clean, followed Him on white horses. (15) Now out of His mouth goes a sharp sword, that with it He should strike the nations'.*

I don't know how long it took to kill this vast army but I can imagine men quite far away watching men dissolve in front of their eyes, knowing instantly they are on the wrong side and that there is absolutely *nothing* they can do about it! It also bears mentioning that Jesus approaches from Petra before going to battle. The blood on His cloak is not from fighting there as He had already arrived with it on His Cloak and I daresay it was His way of saying I was slain to produce my blood forgiveness I will now destroy with blood. To the Jews in Petra it must have been like a flypast of the biggest air force in the world with the Lord checking in on His people and saying "I've got your back!!". Also, the people had to run and walk the two hundred and twenty kilometres (one hundred and thirty miles) to Petra and it says that the land was cleaved open behind them as they went (gullies opened etc) and this would be a parallel with the Israelites fleeing before Pharaoh many centuries before, except on that occasion the water was opened and cleaved shut).

It must be noted that the people of the Earth, at this stage, will open their mouths in horror, knowing full well what is in store for them (Matthew 24:30) 30 '*Then the sign of the Son of Man will appear in Heaven, and then all the tribes of the Earth will mourn, and they will see the Son of Man coming on the clouds of Heaven with power and great glory'.*

In verse 31, He collects his elect from the four corners of the Earth. This scripture has led to a lot of controversy but if you read the Bible simplistically, elect simply means all who have come to know Him during the Tribulation. They are all brought to Israel immediately after Armageddon.

Can you picture the sight of His return? A small glowing light appearing in the supernatural darkness, getting bigger and bigger until it is so massive that a full rotation of the Earth will allow all mankind to see it, full of brightness from Jesus on His white horse and the glow from His soldiers and the Church just behind him! Hallelujah! If this does not excite you I really believe you need to repent of your apathy and look to His coming. It's the only time God gives us a crown; given to those that eagerly await His coming, like the Jewish Bride standing on a dusty path, shielding her eyes against the sun. "Is that the caravan that carries the love of my life? I can't wait to see him, to be held in his strong arms to comfort me and then take me to a place for my wedding!"

We have all seen this with brides on reality TV, squealing with excitement over their pending marriage. CHURCH, WE need to be like that too and if you are not, something is wrong and you need to seek the answer in prayer!

Chapter 9

Questions answered

a) Where is the Church during the Tribulation?

From what we have read so far, you will see that the Bride of Christ, The Church, is in Heaven when the 70th week of Daniel (Tribulation and Great Tribulation) plays out on Earth.

What will they be doing there? Firstly the Church will arrive in new, immortal bodies dressed in white. All the aches, pains and hurts are removed and painful memories of lost loved ones will be wiped away from our tearful eyes by Jesus Himself (Revelation 21: 4). We will see our saved relatives and friends and even former enemies, if redeemed and dance for joy! There will be a LOT of noise and jubilation as we see our dear friends. I also believe we will see people we impacted in our lives and may very well be extremely surprised by the people we meet there, some we may have thought would never be saved. This will be a time of great joy, relief and exultation and as the memories of our lost friends depart from us forever we enter a period of mental peace and joy, with the knowledge of God Himself filling every fibre of our being. Our knowledge will be awesome but never at God's level (1 Corinthians 13:12). We will enjoy long walks along stunning lake shores as we talk in wonder about what has happened and we will stare in awe at our God Who glows brightly.

But before this we have to undergo the Bema seat judgement, which sounds ominous but it is not.

❧ ☙

The Bema Seat judgment and the judgment Seat of Christ are one and the same. The Greek word 'bema' means judgment seat and can be found in the Greek text of Romans 14 :10 and 2 Corinthians 5:10 where it refers to the judgment seat of Christ. This judgment will occur in Heaven just after the Rapture and is explained in 1 Corinthians 3:10-15. Therefore it does not concern our salvation.

In ancient Greece, the Bema seat was the judges stand in the athletic contests. It was where the winners of events were awarded their victory crowns, similar to the medal ceremonies in the modern Olympics. Therefore, many scholars see the bema judgment as the place where newly Raptured believers will receive the crowns they will have earned for the quality of their Christian life on Earth. In 1 Corinthians 9 : 24-27 Paul reminded us that these athletes trained diligently for the games and did so in the hope of winning a crown that would not last. How much more diligently should we train to win crowns that will last forever?

The crowns believers can receive are identified as the Everlasting Crown (Victory) in 1 Corinthians 9:25 the Crown of the Soul Winner in Philippians 4 : 1 and 1 Thessalonians 2:19, the Crown of Righteousness in 2 Timothy 4:8, the Crown of Life in James 1:12 and Revelation 2:10 and the Crown of Glory in 1 Peter 5: 4 .

These crowns are a form of recognition from the Lord, and we are not required to give them back. He doesn't need our crowns or anything else we have. However, we will lay them at His feet as a way of acknowledging that every thing we have accomplished has been at His urging and in His strength. In John 15:5 He said if we remain in Him we'll bear much fruit but apart from Him we can do nothing.

There is one reward, however, that God will give us directly and that is for having earnestly waited for His return to Earth, seeking Him out night and day as a lover does looking at a long road to see if her husband to be is coming toward her.

b) Marriage of the Church

In the parable of the 10 Virgins, the wedding banquet symbolizes the Millennial Kingdom and takes place on Earth. No mention is made of the actual wedding because the people to whom Jesus directed the parable (Tribulation Survivors) will not be present, but since the banquet follows the actual ceremony, it must have been earlier, and since the Lord is just returning, it must have happened in Heaven.

In Revelation 19: 6-9 the tenses of the verbs give us clues as to timing. The wedding 'has come', the bride 'has made herself ready' and fine linen 'was given her'. These are all past tense and hint that the wedding may have already taken place. But then verse 9 pronounces a blessing on those who 'are invited' to the wedding supper. This verse is in the present tense and refers to Tribulation survivors who will soon be welcomed into the Millennial Kingdom. A bride does not receive an invitation to her own wedding banquet, and certainly would not consider it a blessing to be invited. The two passages are in agreement. They imply that the wedding takes place in Heaven, and the banquet (Kingdom) takes place afterward on Earth.

c) The Millennial Kingdom

Jesus is now on the throne in the New Jerusalem, a huge city 1400 miles x 1400 miles that hovers above the Earth. God's elect (the Tribulation saints) will have been brought by angels to Jerusalem. God the Father will be in the temple just north of Jerusalem near modern day Shiloh where animal sacrifices are once again in use by people that populate the Earth in the Millennium. It is only the Church that was saved by grace and animal sacrifice will be the norm going forward. The children born in the Millennium will be reminded of the immense sacrifice Jesus made for them during the sacrificial ceremonies.

The Church or Bride of Christ will work with Jesus to rule the Earth as Kings. This will be conducted from the New Jerusalem but obviously there must be some form of commutation to Earth as the Bible says the glory of the Earth and its riches will be brought to the doors of the New Jerusalem. Similarly we will no doubt visit parts of Earth under our jurisdiction along with angels that help administer edicts and rulings.

It is worthy to note that although all evil people that rejected Christ in the Tribulation period have now been removed from Earth, the people going into the Millennium will have sin nature in them so that by the end of the Millennium, when Satan is released from his chains, he will gather yet another army to try and destroy God as he did previously in the battle of Armageddon (Revelation 20: 7). You would think he would have learned his lesson! The fact that sin will rebound is supported by Psalm 2: 8-9 that says God will rule with a 'rod of iron' during this one thousand year period and God will have to adjudicate, with us, all disagreements that arise, ruling firmly and justly.

I have a bit of morbid curiosity about me judging a problem on Earth as a King when someone tries to kill me for making a ruling they don't like. I guess a knife could not harm me nor a bullet penetrate my skin. But this is just my human brain imagining that! Superman?

During the Millennium it would appear that because God has repaired the Earth to an amazing level, that people will start living very long lives again. It will be tough for Kingdom Saints (not the church) to maintain sacrifices and maintain holy lives but many will fall short and lose their place in the Heavenly

Kingdom. Their names will not be added to the book of life. The Lamb's book of life was written or filled out before creation began and has the name of every person that accepted Christ as their saviour. Even the Millennium believers will be doing this through the daily sacrifice and they will have to work hard to ensure their name is not blotted out of the book. This follows a Jewish custom in Rosh Hashanah where the priest would write a person's name in a book if he had lived an exemplary life in that year and if not, he had ten days to make good before having his name blotted out of the book of life.

I believe it is only the Church and Tribulations saints that will have their names in the Book of life, although Revelation 20: 12 says books were opened as well as the Book of life. You will notice the books (plural) is with a small letter 'b' while the Book of Life is with a capital 'B'. This would infer the other books have records of all the failings and unbelief of all of lost humanity while the Book of life is for people who are saved throughout time. The Church is already made pure and cannot be removed while Tribulation saints would have to make sure their names are *added*.

d) The very last days

In Chapter 20 of Revelation you will see that Satan is freed from his chains in the bottomless pit, to entice nations to fight God's people and attack the throne of God in Jerusalem one more time. I believe he is freed as his final judgement has not taken place yet.

His armies advance on the beloved city (Jerusalem) where God and the Millennial saints are living and there he meets his demise, along with all the armies that Earth could put together, destroyed by fire from Heaven.

The Great White Throne judgement is then held and the believers that are in the Book of Life will dwell with God forever while Satan is thrown into an eternal lake of fire where the beast and false prophet have already been screaming for over a thousand years. Sadly, all of the lost and unregenerate people, after having their records read from the 'other books', are also cast screaming into the lake of fire, where their torment goes on day and night forever. What is wonderful is that Death itself, that horrible thing that entered humanity in the Garden of Eden is also thrown into the Lake of Fire, along with Hades so that mankind will never again experience death.

e) The New Jerusalem

Although the book of Revelation (and indeed the whole Bible) is written in Chronological order, it would appear the arrival of the New Jerusalem happens after the Great White Throne judgement. This obviously can't be the case because it says in Revelation 21:24 that only the nations that are saved may walk into it, inferring there are evil people outside. This can't be the case if the New Jerusalem arrives after all evil are in the Lake of Fire. This is one of several 'telescoping' prophecies that John used, where he starts a theme and then comes back to flesh it out so to speak. The New Jerusalem actually departs from Heaven, with us in it, at the second coming. As it is too massive to land on the Earth it's reasonable to assume it comes close to the Earth. As God's light illumines the New Jerusalem it's possible that will be the source of light for the Earth, which will be in a state of almost complete darkness. This is confirmed in Revelation 21: 23-24.

Many believers will not know and may even be 'saddened' to learn that the New Jerusalem is our eternal home and not Heaven. But if you read the description of it you will be well pleased and lack nothing at all. God will be dwelling with us. There will be no artificial lights as God lights up the whole structure. I see it as a hotel that can move and as it came out of Heaven it must surely be able to go there too. Whatever God has planned is beyond our imagination. One mathematician has estimated, roughly, that if every believer from all time lives in the New Jerusalem we will each have a mansion 182 000 square feet in size. That beats my 3000 square foot home. But I guess we will not need all that space as bedrooms will not be needed and a lot of space will be given to meeting places, dining halls and waterfalls and lakes. How exciting!!

Once the Great White Throne judgement is over and all evil, Hades and death is thrown into the Lake of Fire, the Earth and Heavens will be made new and a renewed Heaven and Earth brought forth. (There is a lot of confusion as to whether our planet Earth and all the Heavens we know are destroyed and new ones made or whether we will see our current Earth made new, cleansed of all sinful objects and decay. I subscribe to the latter for two simple reasons. God did not destroy our planet in the flood, he made it new. Secondly, just as our evil deeds will be burned up, so will the relics of sin and decay be burned up to leave a pure new Earth. The Heavens referred to is our atmosphere, where all pollutants will disappear, leaving a pure and dynamic living planet for us to interact with through all eternity.

f) Resurrections and allocated living places

My studies have led to me to believe the following:

1. Old testament saints that died before Christ rose again went to Paradise. Their flesh remained in the ground. When Jesus was resurrected He took their *spirits*, not their bodies, with Him to Heaven (Ephesians 4: 7-8). This is reflected the first fruits or 'wave offering'. These Saints will be physically resurrected at the end of the Great Tribulation (Revelation 20:4) and given their immortal bodies. They will form part of the new Israel and live there, worshiping God in the renewed Temple of the Millennium just north of Jerusalem in Shiloh. They will form part of the millennial population of Earth.

2. The Orthodox Jews who survive the Great Tribulation will also live in the expanded Israel. They will flee to Petra and by the time Christ appears most if not all will be believers in Him. Those Orthodox Jews who die in the Great Tribulation will be resurrected at the same time as the Old Testament saints. Secular Jews who are not Orthodox believers or new Christians will remain in their graves until the White Throne Judgement.

3. Gentiles that give their lives to Christ in the Great Tribulation but die, will be resurrected at the same time as the Old Testament Jews and Jews from the Great Tribulation (Revelation 6: 9-11; Revelation 20:4; Daniel 12:2). They will become the world nations that inhabit the whole Earth in the Millennium. They will still have a sin nature and their children will either accept or reject God's offer of Salvation, albeit by Old Testament worship practices. They will not be called kings and will therefore serve in some administrative role (Revelation 7: 9-17). Many Bible scholars believe God will give these people a type of 3rd Testament or 'handbook's o know how to become saved in the Millennium. Gentiles believers who survive the Great Tribulation will join their resurrected Gentile Saints populating the nations. Life spans will increase and it will be a time of great plenty but despite this many offspring will reject the way of Truth. They will form the final army that tries to defeat God in the second and last Magog war just before the Great White Throne judgement.

4. The unbelieving dead from all generations including the Millennium period will stay dead until they are resurrected for the Great White Throne judgement, where their sins will be announced before they are thrown screaming into the Lake of Fire for all eternity.

One of the many things that happened in my life to bring me to believing in the Lord was a dream I had as a young man of me being pulled harshly towards this massive steaming, hellish cauldron bursting up from the Earth. The ground was sloped like the top of a funnel and no matter what I did I could not break free from this force pulling me in there. I looked sideways at people and their eyes were wide with fear and they were screaming 'no. no, no!' at the top of their lungs, writhing to break free from this hellish nightmare. The smoke from the fire smelled like Sulphur and it rose with sparks up into an inky black night. I was just about to despair of being lost forever when I turned around and saw a man dressed in glowing white, now quite far off near a tree (symbolic of the cross?). I screamed and pleaded at him for help and as I did so I was immediately released from this vice-like grip pulling me forever down. I ran up the slope rejoicing and then woke up in a bath of sweat.

This dream happened a long time before I read the Bible or even knew anything about the horrors of hell or the joy of Heaven and Salvation. The spirit world is real my friends. When I lived in Pitermaritzburg in South Africa, I went with my pastor to exorcise a Poltergeist from a house. As we arrived in our car, the front door flew open and burning objects came flying out, as if the spirit sensed Christ in us advancing on the home of these two terrified people.

To this day I will never forget the sight I saw in that house. Every single thing that could combust had been burned and it looked as if a laser had been fired at them, with very specific scorch marks here and there. The curtains, pelmets, furniture, carpets, clothes, everything was burnt and the couple with us were in despair and in terror of going home at night. While my pastor stood rooted to the spot with his jaw open I ventured into the house, that being the soldier in me. Every single thing was scorched except in one room and I knew immediately that its contents was where the Poltergeist dwelt. There was a Hindu shrine in that room and not ONE item was damaged at all! I turned back to my pastor and as I passed him I heard a crack and thump noise in the kitchen that I had just walked into. A cupboard door under the sink flew open like in the movies and a jet of flame three feet long surged out of the cupboard. After it subsided I crept forward and looked inside and there was *nothing* inside the cupboard apart from a smouldering home-made hand brush! No chemicals, no electric wires shorting out, just a brush!

I returned to the other four people (their maid had just joined us) and we agreed to break the shrine (which is monumentally hard for a Hindu to do) and for the couple to accept Christ as their Saviour and *not* just another of their 300 million gods. After a small talk explaining there is only One God they readily accepted Him and we broke the shrine to pieces out the back door, praying for the Lord to expel the evil spirit and set His angels about the house for protection. We prayed over every room, anointed their foreheads with oil and left the house. That Poltergeist *never* came back again! That is the same power Christ uses to save and resurrect you! (In case you re asking what happened to the maid, she was already born again and was the one that approached my wife when she heard we were Christians). I can tell you other amazing things I have seen and where God has protected me from death in the military and I am telling you folks, Jesus is ALIVE!!

Chapter 10

Current events that have led up to the Ezekiel nations coming together for war with Israel

Apart from Eschatology (the study of the End Times), I have been very interested in geopolitics for most of my adult life. It has therefore been of the utmost interest for me to watch world events unfold as they have done for the last two decades. There is a clear link between what is happening in the world and the revelation of prophecies made so long ago.

I have been waiting thirty years for Israel to strike oil and they have done so in abundance in the Golan heights although this has been kept quiet (read up on the Genie Corporation – a name suited to keeping news 'in the bottle' so to speak) as well as the Tamar and Levathian gas fields, which are enormous. I believe these are the 'spoils' Russia comes to take in the Ezekiel 38 expedition. More of that just now.

I have also waited a long time for Russia, Turkey and Iran (the main Ezekiel 38 countries) to become allies and a few nights ago when I saw the three leaders shaking hands on the TV I nearly fell off my chair. You see, Erdogan of Turkey is a Sunni and Ali Khamenei of Iran is a Shia. These two sects of Islam hate each other but there they are shaking hands with a beaming Putin right beside them! That is Ezekiel 38 on our television! How close then is the Rapture?

It stands to reason that the real power that will emerge in the near future is Russia with its alliance to China. Russia has to be strong enough to attack Israel in the near future, without worrying about the USA intervening.

Well, why are oil and gas fields so important? The answer to this is Russia's supply of natural gas to Europe. As I type this, the US and Europe are imposing various sanctions on Russia and just a few months ago members of the European Union met to discuss ways of severing Europe's dependence upon Russian natural gas and that ways of finding natural gas elsewhere, including importing it from gas-rich USA, must be looked at. It was quickly determined that shipping natural gas to Europe from the USA would be too expensive although Latvia is building a gas port for liquid gas to come ashore there. Recent news shows that Latvia and Estonia are fed up with expensive natural gas imports from Russia and are building terminals to get their gas from somewhere else.

The one possible scenario now facing us is that sanctions being put on Russia are extended to banning the importation of Russian gas into Europe, which by the way largely enters Europe via the Ukraine, which Russia is now eying, making false claims that ethnic Russians in the Ukraine are being treated badly, as a pretext to a total invasion of the country.

However, for Europe to ban the importation of Russian gas as a sanction against Russia (possibly before or after Russia invades the Ukraine proper), she will have to have reliable and cheaper gas alternatives at hand as Russia supplies just under 40% of Europe's natural gas requirements.

Well, who has one of the biggest natural gas fields in the region? You guessed it, Israel!

Gas discoveries

Field	Discovered	Estimated size
Tamar	2009	10.8 trillion cubic feet
Dalit	2009	700 billion cubic feet
Leviathan	2010	22 trillion cubic feet
Dolphin	2011	81.3 billion cubic feet

The Russian annexation of Crimea and the possible, no, *probable* invasion of Ukraine under the false pretence of assisting ethnic Russians in the east of Ukraine and near Moldova, will almost certainly set the stage for the eventual attack on Israel by Russia and her predominantly Shia allies as she tries to re-set regional natural gas supplies back in Russia's favour. Sanctions put on Iran in November 2018 will drive the Iranian leadership into a frenzy, especially now that they have been removed from the international money payment scheme called SWIFT which will greatly slow down payments to them from international banks. This financial setback will be a major driver pushing Iran deeper into Russia's fold and of course the natural target to vent their fury on will be Israel.

Russia will act reluctantly at first, coming against Israel with 'hooks put in her Jaws' (Ezekiel 38:4), a phrase denoting a degree of unwillingness to begin with. Perhaps moral and military support from China will encourage Russia to 'go all the way' in its attempts to 'take spoil' from Israel. I am waiting for Russia to be sanctioned fully and gas flows into Europe from Israel to be the main trigger for End Times events to really kick in and remember, the USA will be severely weakened from the Rapture and will not be in a position to stop Russia attacking Israel. With China behind her, Russia will have plenty of clout to 'go south'.

We now need to turn to the previous US President (Obama) and the current incumbent, Donald Trump, to see how their governing styles have led to the Ezekiel 38 confederation coming together. It is one twisted, convoluted mess and I'm not sure I will get it 100% correct but I will supply you with an outline that may give you pause for thought.

President Obama

When I spoke at a seminar on 'The truth about Israel' on April 20th 2013, I had one clearly agitated young woman come up to me at the end of the seminar and ask me why I thought Obama was a Muslim when he had clearly indicated he was a Christian in various talk shows in the USA.

I was more aghast at her ignorance than the fact that Obama is indeed a Sunni Muslim. I advised the young lady to take her blinkers off and do some deep research of her own with an open mind.

For the reader, please do your own in-depth study of President Obama and you will quickly see that he is indeed a Sunni Muslim. His foreign policy became quite clear and understandable when you use this matrix as a template for his and the White House's actions in the Muslim world.

However, in case we have some readers that do not want to do their own research, here are a few reasons why I consider him to be a Muslim:-

1. He was raised as Barry Soetero in Indonesia where he studied in a Sunni School.
2. His natural father and step-father were Sunni Muslims.
3. The first leader he contacted after being made President was Abbas, in fact the first four calls were all with regional Arab leaders and although Israel was called too I think that was a sop to make things look balanced and fair. Gone was the first call to the UK Prime Minister and so too the 'special' relationship with the UK.
4. He rarely took Michelle Obama with him to Muslim countries. This is a sure sign of following Islamic protocol.
5. He apologised for the USA in his first international speech in Cairo, a Muslim majority country.
6. He has systematically allowed Sunni radicals to get into power from the

west coast of Africa to The Yemen while studiously avoiding assistance to any Shia nation or tribe or government, even ending Bush's war in Iraq that supported the Shia majority.

7. Mr Obama has steadfastly refused any help to Christians being killed in Egypt, Syria, Nigeria, South Sudan or in the far east. Barely a word of condemnation has left his lips for any anti-Christian atrocity anywhere in the world.

8. He bent over backwards to get the Moslem Brotherhood into office in Egypt, even continuing with £1.5 billion dollars in aid to a known terrorist group that helped bring the twin towers down. When the current military booted the Muslim Brotherhood out of office Mr Obama threatened to cancel US aid to Egypt and tried no less than twenty times to get the Egyptian military to bow to his demands. Fortunately, the head of the Egyptian army is a US trained soldier and knows the Americans well. He resisted all demands for the reinstatement of the Moslem Brotherhood and has been boosted in this effort by a $10 billion dollar loan from Qatar and various emirate countries.

9. Mr Obama appointed many Muslims into high-ranking offices in the US and changed the wording on the 'war against terror'. He also appointed anti-Semites to almost every major office in the US government, like Hagel and Perry for example.

10. He insisted on civilian trials of terrorists because he knew that the civilian system may well get the terrorist off charges or at least offer him better living conditions if found guilty.

11. Mr Obama has publicly stated that there is nothing sweeter than the sound of Muslims being called to prayer in the mornings. What an odd statement for a Christian to make!

12. Mr Obama made it very easy for Muslims to enter the USA as refugees.

13. He cut short the war in Iraq, wasting all that US blood, because Shias were now in power and he did not want to support their longevity.

14. Mr Obama similarly increased support for the Sunni government in Afghanistan during setbacks.

15. He bowed to the Saudi King, something only adherents to Sunni Islam would do.

There are many other reasons that will convince the reader that Mr Obama is a Muslim of the Sunni sect. And just in case you counter these assertions with other public statements he may have made to the contrary, just remember Muslims are allowed to lie under a system called Taqiyyah that enables them to gain an advantage or curry favour with an infidel.

The other half of Mr Obama

There is also Mr Obama the private individual. Who is this man that no-one ever heard of prior to his election to the most powerful office in the world? He was a nobody before the political elites decided he was the right man for their plans for the future. Mr Obama had achieved virtually nothing in Congress, achieved little academically, was wayward in his youth and heavily influenced by the writings of Saul Alinsky, a left wing radical of note. Indeed, one of the reasons he chose Hillary Clinton as Secretary of State is that she too was a staunch Alinskiite. For those readers that know nothing about Saul Alinsky's teachings please read up on him and you will start to understand Obama's internal US policies. Also read up on the Fabian society.

He also got a Nobel peace prize, for doing what? Shouting, 'we need change?' I think even Mr Obama's supporters feel this was done to try and turn him into some type of messiah.

There is no doubt in my mind that Mr Obama is a very left-wing radical and if the reader studies Mr Obama's internal policies and the 10 tenets of Marxism you will quickly discover they are almost the same.

The reason why Obama was the *perfect* choice for the political elites is that he is a Muslim. I will not go into this subject now, as this book is meant to be simple in its presentation, but there is no doubt whatsoever that western political elites, through social engineering and mass immigration of Muslims into the west, has set in motion the perfect storm of using and financing Islamic radicals to achieve the goals of the political elites; the elimination of Judeo-Christian laws, statutes and morals, which are complete anathema to their way of thinking. This is one of the reasons why the deliberate promotion of Islam in the West is so profound and why Muslims are treated like sacred cows in western countries. It is a deliberate plan. (Folks, I wrote this Chapter in 2013 – prophetically referring to a Muslim invasion of Europe in 2015).

As part of the Fabian tactic (named after a Roman General called Fabius Maximus, who wore down his enemy by attrition), morals are being ground away and homosexuality promoted as the new-found lifestyle. This suits the political elite, as it destroys the Judeo-Christian fabric of society they hate, but is oddly a contradiction to their Islamic storm troopers who also hate homosexuality and for this reason the Muslim 'tool' will be eliminated in due course.

This means that the Marxist-Leninist political elites that rule behind the scenes in this world, will use Islam to bring in changes that could not ordinarily be brought in during peace times, like the Patriot Act in the USA and will allow control and dictatorship over the Western masses like never before. This has also resulted in the tapping and snooping on phones, social networks and other forms of communication. It will also bring in all sorts of control over the media and social networks like Twitter, Facebook and so on where you will see a marginalization of right wing networks and thought.

Universities will push all students to become politically correct zombies that cannot think for themselves, using all sorts of hurts and worries and social injustice to push, sometimes violently, for their demands to be met.

The terror of radical Islam is the perfect tool to bring in the top-down government dictatorship that the political elites desire. The profound feeling of terror among the far left that Obama almost lost his second term in office is a clear indication that Mr Obama's 'change, yes we can' is to turn the USA into a socialist dictatorship using Islam as its fear-creating tool for change.

One of the last bastions of resistance to this change is the US constitution and this is the reason why the elites have appointed 'Czars' to sidestep it. Laws were being ignored or moulded to suit the elites. And the biggest stumbling block to them is the 2nd amendment, the right to bear arms.

The elites, including Obama himself, the rent-a-crowd radicals and ignorant people all believe that ridding the civilian population of weapons will make the population safe from crazies are at the forefront of trying to disarm America. They ignore, or do not realise, that where this has happened in every country on Earth, with few exceptions, said countries have succumbed to dictatorship and high levels of gun crime.

This happened in Germany when Hitler disarmed its population, in Russia, as well as several South American counties. Knife crime rose 300% when guns were banned in Australia and crime in general rose 1000% in South Africa. Knife crime is now at horrific levels in London.

Why am I talking so much about America and what has it to do with the end times?

1. Firstly, it's an indication that the USA will not participate as a nation in the end times. For the only world superpower to not enter scripture in the pivotal days we are living in is amazing. I believe the ordering of

thousands of armoured cars and billions of rounds of ammunition by the Department of Homeland security a couple of years ago indicates that a civil war is about to break out in the US. This will weaken the US to a point where she will not have the finance to wage war in various 'end-times' battles.

2. A paradigm shift is taking place in the USA as socialist policies and illegal immigration bankrupt America. I believe this may replace Islam as the tool to bring change.

3. The military sequestration that happened under Obama has thankfully been overturned by Trump but was planned to make the USA weak enough to be unable to fend off a Chinese invasion.

4. US aircraft carriers were foolishly stacked in a few ports that made them inviting targets to either the Russians or Chinese, or both operating under the burgeoning Shanghai treaty countries.

5. America's elitist policies will help the rise of Islam that will in turn destroy the very Judeo-Christian principles upon which it was founded. This will also help create a world-wide ecumenical church that weds itself to Islam, becoming the 'Harlot that rides the beast' (Revelation 17).

The elites' election victory of Obama set the stage for American decline and the launch of a church that blends with radical Islam. This is why Mr Obama's presence was so profound for the world and will still result in the way of life as we know it being changed forever. And if you think what he and his sponsors have done in the USA only applies to the USA, then look to Great Britain, Australia and Europe as examples of how these policies have taken root there; the community organization concept (1st step in communism) is big in Britain and all of Europe is awash with 50 million Muslims who are treated as holy cows in any dispute, to the cost of Christians and Jews alike. Homosexual marriage is just about accepted in all countries and weird churches like Chrislam are taking root. Next will be the legalization of incest in my opinion.

If you think the New World order is a conspiracy joke, start doing some serious study!

Back To Events That Transpired Under Obama's Rule

Through acts of commission and omission, which are too many to expand on here, the world started to see the US as a weak and fractured country. It unleashed many tyrants to have a go at doing things their way (North Korea became more active for example, Iran too).

One of the biggest failures of Obama was not executing the 'thin red line' he had promised over the gassing of Syrian government opponents. This sealed his fate as a weak leader and his appalling response to the US ambassador getting killed in Libya made people sit up and scratch their heads. I personally believe the ambassador was about to reveal that weapons from Libya were being smuggled through Turkey and being given to the Free Syrian army 'moderates' who actually gave a lot of these weapons to Al Qaida/Al Nusra and also to ISIS. I am of the opinion that the USA under Obama used ISIS to counter the Shia expansion into Iraq and Syria and may be the reason that many US pilots returned to base with no bombs dropped in their campaign against ISIS militants and that Turkey allowed oil from ISIS controlled areas to move freely into Turkey. Many unsavoury dealings took place when Obama finally decided to make a deal with Iran over her nuclear abilities, freeing over $150 billion dollars of frozen funds for Iran to use building up its military. The Iranians laughed all the way to the bank and allowed inspectors to look at their nuclear facilities in part, while handing all their research to North Korea to make and test nuclear bombs for them! Trump, thankfully, has seen through all that. The only reason I can think of as to why Obama let Shia Iran off the hook is that he wanted a legacy of him being a high statesman and a man of peace but also because I think he has a distinct dislike for Israel and would not resist a war between the two countries.

The Arab Spring started under Obama's watch and it was a wonderful opportunity for America to support struggling populations that wanted to get rid of harsh rulers and introduce some form of democracy. But what did Obama do? Nothing! This resulted in radicals sweeping into all the nations of north Africa, the Levant, Yemen and partly Iraq. By default the old 'Kings of the South' were now under Sunni radicals.

Iran, freed from the restraint of a strong US government now started out on a very brave foreign expedition all of its own, sending troops to Syria and Iraq and bolstering Hezbollah both financially and militarily.

Turkey in the meantime started to play Devil's advocate. Wedged between Russia and Syria and now Iran, she had to make some choices about who to support. But Erdogan, the leader of secular Turkey needed power and wanted to become more Islamic (Turkey desires to be the head of the Muslim Sunni Caliphate). So Erdogan faked a coup in July 2016 saying that it was a cleric called Gulan in America that was responsible for the coup but to me it looked so fake and too much of a false flag scenario to be taken seriously. It did, however, allow

Erdogan to get rid of many military leaders, civil servants (up to 60 000) and intellectuals and newspapers that criticized him, thus firmly taking the power out of the military's hands and putting it almost solely into his.

Turkey continued to find itself in an awkward position. It is fighting the Kurds in the east, who are supported by the USA (which effectively makes the USA an enemy) but supports the USA in Nato, while supporting Russia in the West in its dealings with Iran and Syria, but opposing Russia and Syria in the Idlib Provence where it supports so-called 'moderate' free Syrian fighters, many of whom are big bushy-bearded men belonging to Al Nusra and dregs of ISIS.

Could anyone make this up? It is so complicated. But to cut a long story short, Turkey is outwardly allies with Iran and Russia while supporting America in NATO. We know from prophecy, however, that Turkey will eventually follow Russia and Iran against Israel. Her heart has been hardened against the USA due to sanctions. Trump has put tariffs on Turkey's steel exports which are no doubt linked to the freeing of pastor Andrew Brunson who has been held in Turkey for nearly two years. But despite his release the sanctions remain. Turkey's currency is in free-fall.

So, as we stand, the 'Kings of the North' are now filled with mainly Shia Islam and the 'Kings of the South' are Sunni. But the most serious thing we face is that the countries which make up the Ezekiel 38 alliance are all bankrupt, apart from Russia, but the loss of her gas exports will weaken her dreadfully and remember what Hitler did to motivate his people and take their minds off empty bellies, he took them to war!

To conclude the section on Obama and his radical ideas, please note that I do not include sensible and intelligent Democrats (or is that an oxymoron?) in this scenario, being law abiding people that merely want a better deal for everyone, I refer mainly to the radical left who are extremely dangerous.

The mainstream media, fake news and false flags

One of the most profound impacts on modern day life is the ability of news organizations to influence the masses without really realizing what is happening to them. With the exception of one or two news outlets in America and even less in the remaining western world, all media is now spawned by the left, either moderate or radical. This is having a profound effect on how students think and people in general. It has led to a firestorm of argument, some of it full of hatred, between left and right wing contributors to social media like Twitter, Facebook and many other platforms. I have been aghast at how supposedly ethical and unbiased outlets have taken news clips and presented them totally out of context, thus creating a false impression of the target or 'victim'.

This scenario is now so rampant that fake news is becoming the truth of the day. The elite have come to realise that 'False Flag' scenarios like the 'weapons of mass destruction' in Iraq, the 'twin towers debacle' and 'Russia-gate' leave far too much evidence behind to be safe for political gain anymore. The obvious conclusion is to remove false flags and replace them with fake news which is almost impossible to verify or neutralise once the public has got their teeth into it. For this reason, major news outlets that are threatened with low readership, ratings and closure are in some cases generating fake news that inflames the reader, encouraging them to buy more newspapers or select news outlets that fit only *their* viewpoint. Remember, Satan is the father of lies and he uses lies and fakery very effectively to turn audiences in his direction, which in this case is ultimately Israel but as America is her strongest patron, Satan will have to deal with the USA anyway he can. Destroy the male, destroy family values, push division and drugs, race wars etc etc and have a field day with abortion although I am glad to say that Satan fails when it comes to killing off babies as they automatically go to be with the Lord.

President Trump

The year 2016 saw the election of probably the most controversial President in US history. The left-right, pro-Socialist division that Obama worked so hard to produce in his eight years in office and the black-white racial split came full ball out of the planning rooms of the Socialists and Marxists; not because Trump encouraged it, but this man, who was not one of theirs, was not part of the 'swamp' and could not be bought was the ideal target to swing into action against after eight years of rehearsal. Trump was *their* catalyst to accelerate far left liberal ideology based on Alinsky's teachings, the ten steps of Communism and Marxism although their overall manifesto says they want to combat racism, sexism and any form of injustice.

However, although injustice, racism and sexism occurs on both sides of the political divide, the perpetrators of almost all of the social unrest have come from the left, whom these ideologues support in the forms of groups like:-

1. *Antifa* (anti-fascist [sic]) (Antifa is a black-clad, bandanna and helmet-wearing group of self-described anarchists and revolutionary communists known for violence and threats. The name Antifa is short for 'anti-fascists'

which is a joke as they are surely fascist in their behaviour. They have become a regular presence at anti-Trump rallies across the U.S. that often turn violent. Their leadership is not widely known but you can bet a well known left wing philanthropist is lurking there somewhere).

2. *Black Lives Matter* (This movement congealed around two fatal incidents: the first, the shooting to death of Trayvon Martin in 2012; the second, the shooting to death of Michael Brown in 2014. The elites support this movement and have encouraged its spread because it guarantees support for the Democrats. I do not believe the Democrats give a fig about Black Lives [when you look at their racist history] and only want their votes. There is strong evidence that when Brown was shot, people who took part in the days of riots that followed were paid to do so. Brown was no innocent puppy either. He was well known as a bully and had just robbed a store shortly before being shot. Evidence, given by black witnesses, confirmed that he did indeed attack the police officer that shot him).

3. *Workers World Party* (Members of the Workers World Party, a hard-core Marxist-Leninist group, have appeared at anti-monument and anti-Trump events across America. The party was founded in 1959 by a group led by Sam Marcy of the Socialist Workers Party. It has supported the Weather Underground Organization and had a strong presence in the Black Lives Matter movement).

4. *Colour of change* (One group that has attacked President Trump and advocated for removing Confederate symbols across America is Colour of Change, a non profit organization that was co-founded by President Obama's former green-jobs 'czar', Van Jones and James Rucker).

5. *Onward together* (Launched by Hillary Clinton in May 2017 after her failed bid for the White House, Onward Together is a political action organization that seeks to be 'part of the resistance' against President Trump by funding many of the leftist activists organizing against the administration).

6. *Indivisible* (Indivisible is a national anti-Trump movement that often targets members of Congress and calls for resistance against the Trump administration. It's a collection of leftist activist groups totalling 5,900 chapters that have popped up across America since Trump's election. One of its campaigns targeted Republican efforts to repeal Obamacare.

7. *Move On.org* (MoveOn.org, is a far left group funded by billionaire George Soros, claiming eight million members across America, was launched in

1998 with a campaign of opposition to the impeachment of President Bill Clinton and emerged as a fundraising vehicle for Democratic Party candidates. Today, it is focused on pushing the impeachment of Trump. That's how far MoveOn.org has moved on in 19 years).

8. *By Any Means Necessary BAMN* (By Any Means Necessary, or BAMN, has been in the middle of quite a bit of the worst violence in recent months. In February 2018, BAMN helped organize the fiery riots that resulted in the cancellation of a speech by Milo Yiannopoulos at the University of California at Berkeley. In a statement to NBC News, UC Berkeley said: 'The violence was instigated by a group of about 150 masked agitators who came onto campus and interrupted an otherwise non-violent protest.' The speech was cancelled 'amid violence, destruction of property and out of concern for public safety,' according to the university, and 1,500 people reportedly surrounded the venue. Rioters threw firebombs and commercial-grade fireworks at police. They slammed a metal barricade against a door of the building).

9. *Ultraviolet (Soros)* (UltraViolet is part of a network of organizations that called for CEOs to resign from Trump's business council. The group received $65 000 from MoveOn.org in 2016. MoveOn.org is a far left group funded by billionaire George Soros).

10. *Industrial Workers of the World*; Organizing for Action (Obama). (Members of the Industrial Workers of the World – a Chicago-based organization of socialists, anarchists and Marxists – clashed with police on May 20 2018 while protesting a permitted remembrance of 'Confederate Memorial Day' in Graham, North Carolina. Three IWW protesters who were armed with knives were arrested. A protester grabbed a flag, presumably a Confederate banner, according to reports, and tried to rip it up).

Doesn't this jolly lot sound akin to the 10 tenets of Communism?:-

1. Abolition of property in land and application of all rents of land to public purposes.
2. A heavy progressive or graduated income tax (The Democrats will raise taxes if elected).
3. Abolition of all rights of inheritance.
4. Confiscation of the property of all emigrants and rebels (Christians, Jews

and right wing people will fall into this category).

5. Centralisation of credit in the hands of the state, by means of a national bank with State capital and an exclusive monopoly. (It will be modelled on the Socialist Bank of North Dakota).

6. Centralisation of the means of communication and transport in the hands of the State.

7. Extension of factories and instruments of production owned by the State; the bringing into cultivation of waste-lands, and the improvement of the soil generally in accordance with a common plan.

8. Equal liability of all to work. Establishment of industrial armies, especially for agriculture (Has failed miserably all over the world).

9. Combination of agriculture with manufacturing industries; gradual abolition of all the distinction between town and country by a more equable distribution of the populace over the country (has failed everywhere).

10. Free education for all children in public schools. Abolition of children's factory labour in its present form. Combination of education with industrial production, &c, &c.

Why does this matter?

As the USA is the last true Super Power of the world, it is very important to follow what is going on inside that country, for several reasons. Firstly, will America be around to support Israel in the end times and if not, why not? Secondly it's my opinion that the New World Order that wants a One World Government and one religion and if possible only one race on Earth plus a highly reduced population, is more likely to come through the lawlessness of the extreme left than the right, which is much more conservative in nature.

Bearing this in mind, the demise of conservative America is absolutely critical to the advancement of the invisible hand that wants global domination, Satan himself. Yes, there are people on the right who want this plan to succeed also but it is the vehicle of the left that has been chosen to bring it about.

Satan's plan is to destroy mankind and what appears to be ten organizations in the USA that want to resist racism, sexism and injustice have in fact been corrupted by this wily, ages old enemy to destroy the very foundations of humanity they want to 'help'. And, using the tactics of Fabianism (and Fabianism itself) have incrementally destroyed what was considered normal and healthy for many centuries, namely marriage between a man and woman only; the sanctity of the human body (God's temple) through wilful abortion and the leadership of a family unit by a male. Hollywood has played a major part in destroying the male and the traditional family unit and you will find most supporters of the ten organizations listed above fall into this category. It is no accident, it is designed and propels forth from the cradle to the Universities where liberal groups have a 'field day' destroying young lives, confusing them with their warped and godless ideology. Any opposition is violently opposed with vociferous, loud chanting which cannot be reasoned with. These people *cannot* be reasoned with and the idea of having a debate with them is impossible but for a very few extremely clever and brave people.

I am not going to hide the fact that America is fighting for its survival right now. I believe it has only remained a bastion of light because of its staunch support for Israel but as these Marxist groups grow in power they will undermine '*The Israeli Jews*' at every turn. Can the reader discern what I am saying? Supporting the radical left is supporting death itself. I can guarantee if Hillary Clinton had won the US Presidency the world would be at war with Russia (to keep the Rothschild banks operating there) and the policies of the ten organizations listed above would be implemented full steam ahead. You need to realise that their leaders do not care one jot for people, they *only* want power. This is why black people in the US fester in dying cities while promised the world, given food stamps and then thrown under the bus after elections.

Enter Donald Trump

We all witnessed the miraculous election victory of Donald Trump, propelled into power by one expression foolishly spouted by Hillary Clinton ... .'The deplorables'.

The so-called 'elites' who hold power and are by and large rich and politically very well connected, have risen to a level where they actually think they are better than the rest of humanity. Indeed, their 'Agenda 21' programme plans to kill all but 500 million people who will be serf-like slaves that will satisfy their every whim.

Hillary Clinton is one of the worst 'elites' with many, many dubious financial and political dealings in her and her husband's lifetime. She has risen so far above the everyday person that she has lost contact with them. Yes, she gets involved in many humanitarian deeds but this is by and large for political capital. However, she forgot the 'deplorable' are human beings with lives and jobs and families. In many cases the backbone of America; black, white, Hispanic, Japanese, Chinese and so on. They are your plumbers, carpenters, railroad workers, teachers, janitors, welders, steel workers, construction workers and occupy many other less glamorous but vital occupations. I would like to see Hillary survive without a plumber when her toilet gets backed up. But she will *use* the plumber, she will *use* the carpenter etc but that's as far as her and the elites will go. By default, left-leaning Hollywood and the mainstream media have been given a free pass into this lofty world although the former are just people who still use the toilet!

Big mistake Hillary! The peasants you despise voted you out. Thank God for the constitution that protects people and their right to vote and is one of the main reasons the 'elite' want to usurp or destroy its statutes.

Trump

While Trump says many hurried and irrational things on Twitter, I believe his statements come from a good heart. I believe he knows his faults and is by and large a good man. He is not as proud as many suggest for how many world leaders would allow Christians to openly pray for him while his head is bowed? The left will argue he does this to curry favour with the Bible belt where he draws massive support but he is the only US President in recent US history that has actively helped Christians rather than the sacred cows of Islam.

I genuinely believe that Trump is a Patriot that loves the USA which contradicts his predecessor apologising to the world for America's arrogance while talking in Cairo. Trump has set about making America great again after the very poor domestic performance offered by Obama.

Below are the 12 categories and 81 wins cited by the White House.

Jobs and the economy
- Passage of the tax reform bill providing $5.5 billion in cuts and repealing the Obamacare mandate.
- Increase of the GDP above 3 percent.
- Creation of 1.7 million new jobs, cutting unemployment to 4.1 percent.
- Saw the Dow Jones reach record highs.
- A rebound in economic confidence to a 17-year high.
- A new executive order to boost apprenticeships.
- A move to boost computer sciences in Education Department programmes.
- Prioritizing women-owned businesses for some $500 million in SBA loans.

Killing job-stifling regulations

- Signed an Executive Order demanding that two regulations be killed for every new one creates. He beat that big and cut 16 rules and regulations for every one created, saving $8.1 billion.
- Signed 15 congressional regulatory cuts.
- Withdrew from the Obama-era Paris Climate Agreement, ending the threat of environmental regulations. (Author – humans only produce .006% of greenhouse gases. This is nothing but a tax. However, pollution IS a very serious problem, especially in the oceans).
- Signed an Executive Order cutting the time for infrastructure permit approvals.
- Eliminated an Obama rule on streams that Trump felt unfairly targeted the coal industry.

Fair trade

- Made good on his campaign promise to withdraw from the Trans-Pacific Partnership which was heavily skewered against the USA.
- Opened up the North American Free Trade Agreement for talks to better the deal for the U.S. (Now successful).
- Worked to bring companies back to the U.S., and companies like Toyota, Mazda, Broadcom Limited, and Foxconn announced plans to open U.S. plants.
- Worked to promote the sale of U.S products abroad.
- Made enforcement of U.S. trade laws, especially those that involve national security, a priority.
- Ended Obama's deal with Cuba.

Boosting U.S. energy dominance

- The Department of Interior, which has led the way in cutting regulations, opened plans to lease 77 million acres in the Gulf of Mexico for oil and gas drilling.
- Trump travelled the world to promote the sale and use of U.S. energy.
- Expanded energy infrastructure projects like the Keystone XL Pipeline snubbed by Obama (It's ironic that the unwashed Green people shout and chant against new energy sources and then get in huge SUVs with gas guzzling engines and drive away in them!)
- Ordered the Environmental Protection Agency to kill Obama's Clean Power Plan.
- EPA is reconsidering Obama rules on methane emissions.

Protecting the U.S. homeland
- Laid out new principles for reforming immigration and announced plans to end 'chain migration,' which lets one legal immigrant to bring in dozens of family members.
- Made progress to build the border wall with Mexico.
- Ended the Obama-era 'catch and release' of illegal immigrants.
- Boosted the arrest of illegal migrants inside the U.S.
- Doubled the number of counties participating with Immigration and Customs Enforcement charged with deporting illegals.
- Removed 36 percent more criminal gang members than in fiscal 2016.
- Started the end of the Deferred Action for Childhood Arrival program.
- Ditto for other amnesty programs like Deferred Action for Parents of Americans.
- Cracking down on some 300 sanctuary cities that defy ICE but still get federal dollars.
- Added some 100 new immigration judges.

Protecting communities
- Justice announced grants of $98 million to fund 802 new policemen.
- Justice worked with Central American nations to arrest and charge 4,000 MS-13 members.
- Homeland rounded up nearly 800 MS-13 members, an 83 percent one-year increase.
- Signed three executive orders aimed at cracking down on international criminal organizations.
- Attorney General Jeff Sessions created new National Public Safety Partnership, a cooperative initiative with cities to reduce violent crimes.

Accountability
- Trump has nominated 73 federal judges and won his nomination of Neil Gorsuch to the Supreme Court.
- Ordered ethical standards including a lobbying ban.
- Called for a comprehensive plan to reorganize the executive branch.
- Ordered an overhaul to modernize the digital government.
- Called for a full audit of the Pentagon and its spending.

Combating opioids

- First, the president declared a Nationwide Public Health Emergency on opioids.
- His Council of Economic Advisors played a role in determining that overdoses are underreported by as much as 24 percent.
- The Department of Health and Human Services laid out a new five-point strategy to fight the crisis.
- Justice announced it was scheduling Fentanyl substances (pain killers) as a drug class under the Controlled Substances Act.
- Justice started a fraud crackdown, arresting more than 400.
- The administration added $500 million to fight the crisis.
- On National Drug Take Back Day, the Drug Enforcement Agency collected 456 tons of opioids.

Protecting life

- In his first week, Trump reinstated and expanded the Mexico City Policy that blocks some $9 billion in foreign aid being used for abortions.
- Worked with Congress on a bill overturning an Obama regulation that blocked states from de-funding abortion providers.
- Published guidance to block Obamacare money from supporting abortion (Life begins at conception not when the head leaves the womb which is a liberal concept, allowing abortion up to the time of giving birth. Disgusting).

Helping veterans

- Signed the Veterans Accountability and Whistleblower Protection Act to allow senior officials in the Department of Veterans Affairs to fire failing employees and establish safeguards to protect whistleblowers.
- Signed the Veterans Appeals Improvement and Modernization Act.
- Signed the Harry W. Colmery Veterans Educational Assistance Act, to provide support.
- Signed the VA Choice and Quality Employment Act of 2017 to authorize $2.1 billion in additional funds for the Veterans Choice Program.
- Created a VA hotline.
- Had the VA launch an online 'Access and Quality Tool,' providing veterans with a way to access wait time and quality of care data.
- With VA Secretary Dr. David Shulkin, announced three initiatives to expand access to healthcare for veterans using tele-health technology.

Promoting peace through strength

- Directed the rebuilding of the military and ordered a new national strategy and nuclear posture review.
- Worked to increase defence spending.
- Empowered military leaders to 'seize the initiative and win,' reducing the need for a White House sign off on every mission.
- Directed the revival of the National Space Council to develop space war strategies.
- Elevated U.S. Cyber Command into a major war-fighting command.
- Withdrew from the U.N. Global Compact on Migration, which Trump saw as a threat to borders.
- Imposed a travel ban on nations that lack border and anti-terrorism security.
- Saw ISIS lose virtually all of its territory.
- Pushed for strong action against global outlaw North Korea and its development of nuclear weapons.
- Announced a new Afghanistan strategy that strengthens support for U.S. forces at war with terrorism.
- NATO increased support for the war in Afghanistan.
- Approved a new Iran strategy plan focused on neutralizing the country's influence in the region.
- Ordered missile strikes against a Syrian airbase used in a chemical weapons attack.
- Prevented subsequent chemical attacks by announcing a plan to detect them better and warned of future strikes if they were used.
- Ordered new sanctions on the dictatorship in Venezuela.

Restoring confidence in and respect for America

- Trump won the release of Americans held abroad, often using his personal relationships with world leaders.
- Made good on a campaign promise to recognize Jerusalem as the capital of Israel.
- Conducted a historic 12-day trip through Asia, winning new cooperative deals. On the trip, he attended three regional summits to promote American interests.
- He travelled to the Middle East and Europe to build new relationships with leaders.
- Travelled to Poland and on to Germany for the G-20 meeting where he pushed again for funding of women entrepreneurs

Trump's foreign policy in more detail

While it has been an eye-opening exercise to reveal what Trump has achieved, it is obvious that left wing citizens mainly fight for traditional 'green' subjects like the environment (one of the 10 steps to Communism), women and minority rights, sexual identity and race. I am sure very few far left liberals have even read the list above nor would they even care to. The fact that Trump has brought 6 Trillion dollars back to America, which is impacting their lives directly and indirectly, they want none of it and will not give thanks where it is due. Amazingly, however, CNN, Trump's arch media enemy recently admitted that his financial policies are doing well for America.

It is his foreign policy, however, that is at the heart of this chapter. It goes without saying that the USA does not appear to intervene or even be around when the Magog armies invade Israel, so what has happened to her, the last great superpower that currently loves Israel?

My theories are:

1. The Rapture severely weakens the USA.
2. There is a civil war that paralyses the country.
3. Trump loses office and is replaced by a radical anti-Semite

You see, the *only way* that the world population, including Israel, will recognize God's hand in protecting Israel in the Ezekiel 38 event is the complete absence of any help from other countries.

I am very sad to say that options 2 and 3 are probably what is going to happen. President Trump may well be a one term President, not because of his failings or Democrat successes but because God will allow him to be taken out the way through the voting box. The very shock the liberals suffered at his victory, that caused endless tears and head-scratching for them, is the same pain we conservatives will feel when he is removed by a virtual nobody who espouses the most terrible domestic and foreign policies in their manifesto. The Earth has to be in a state of moral, political and religious decay when this profound prophecy in Ezekiel happens.

Trump's foreign policies will cement once and for all how the world stands when the Russian, Turkish and Iranian tanks roll, with many tens of thousands of troops. It should be pointed out that even if God did not intervene it would be no pushover for the invading armies as Israel is currently the 11th strongest military power on Earth and with its superbly trained troops and high technical ability it could hold its own for a long time.

Nato

In Trump's first meeting with NATO heads of state in July 2018, the leaders were shocked and perplexed to hear that NATO must pay its way and that the headquarters building erected at a cost of $1.4 billion dollars was a waste of money and that it should have been spent on arms. He declared that if NATO members were not prepared to up their contributions to 2% of GDP the United States would have to reconsider its commitment to protecting Europe. This was a far cry from the smiles and handshakes of the Obama period, where he was decimating US military strength to such a high degree that the US may not have been able to help Europe in a war anyway. Trump's comments had their desired effect and NATO is now being financed more evenly. In the end times this will have the desired effect of keeping Europe quite strong, perhaps too strong for Russia to attack but strong enough to form alliances with the Antichrist.

Iran

Iran was given a silver plate with $150 billion of released funds on it by the Obama Administration when he signed an agreement with Iran that was supposed to ensure visibility and honesty with its nuclear programme, which the Iranians offered and Obama accepted, only for Iran to send its scientists and research to North Korea for them to build their bombs, the technology for which North Korea could keep.

Thankfully Trump has seen through this and cancelled the nuclear deal with Iran. This has enraged the Iranians even further, effectively returning them to the pariah state it always has been. To hurt the US they are attacking US-backed Saudi forces fighting the Houthi rebels in Yemen who follow the Shia sect.

Turkey

As stated earlier, Turkey has been playing the Devils advocate by supporting both Russia and the United states while opposing their proxies at the same time. Sanctions Trump put on Turkey's steel exports has, among other pressures, caused the Turkish Lira to drop in value by over 20%. Turkey has tried to get Qatar and Saudi Arabia to help bank roll them but the death of the journalist Khashoggi and Turkey's willingness to expose how he had been killed in the Iranian Embassy in Ankara (Turkey) has caused the Saudi Royal family to withhold financial support for Turkey and being proud humans the Saud Royal family will remember Turkeys folly for a long time to come. The end time result of this is that Turkey, like Iran, is now firmly imbedded with the Russians.

Saudi Arabia

The House of Saud, the ruling Royal family, snubbed Obama for dealing with Iran in a positive light but when Trump came along they saw a golden opportunity to support him in return for many financial and political benefits. Trump was given a royal welcome and invited to partake in the sword dance which is normally reserved for very high ranking members and the House of Saud only. In return Trump saw lucrative defence deals and a strong ally against Iran, in addition to supporting a new friend of Israel. The end time consequences of this is that Saudi Arabia, a strong opponent of Iran, will not be sucked into the Ezekiel Troika. The embarrassment felt by Saudi Arabia over the death of the journalist Khashoggi, willingly revealed by Turkey, has further alienated them from Russia, Turkey and her nemesis Iran.

Russia.

This vast country will become hard hit by US/European sanctions and its inability to sell its natural gas to anyone other than China and maybe India in coming years and will certainly look for a way to hurt the West and Israel.

China

At present China is a very cash-rich country despite abject poverty in many rural areas and is rapidly expanding its military and economic base and influence. However, China is relatively poor in natural resources and for this reason she is buying up huge parts of the world where natural resources abound and if not outright buying them, getting the goods in very lopsided deals that favour them. This makes China very vulnerable and Trump knows this. In order to check China's growing influence, Trump has put tariffs on large portions of China's exports to the United States, which although are not biting now, as the tariffs only come into effect at the end of 2018, will do so in 2019.

I am of the opinion that there is a deeper reason to Trump sanctioning China than mere economics. China is, after all, the only major player that can influence North Korea's leader Kim Jong-un and get him to destroy the very nuclear weapons that he was developing for himself and his buddy Ali Khamenei of Iran. By putting China's 'proverbials' in a vice, Trump has shut down North Korea and firmly kept China in second place economically.

It goes without saying that China remains very vulnerable as America's massive naval fleet could quite easily stop all ships bound with raw materials headed for China, from ever entering its waters. China knows this and was one reason why China joined hands with Russia in the 1992 Shanghai treaty organization, making her a good choice, along with India, for the manpower that the Antichrist needs in the Great Tribulation.

A thought about Trump

It has occurred to the author that just as Muslims know there has to be a state of chaos in the world, with Israel obliterated, before their Mhadi can arrive, so too with Trump. Is it feasible that the 'evangelicals' whispering in his ear know that the Ezekiel 38 event will lead to the return of Christ and perhaps consciously or unconsciously are moulding Trump's foreign policy to accelerate this process? We will never know.

Satan's ingress into the Church

This is a very big subject and needs a lot of study by the reader. The biggest enemies the Church is facing today are *apathy, humanism and false doctrine.* Slowly but surely large Church organizations in their quest for more and more members have allowed humanism to creep in where works are more important than Christ. Yes, works are important but *only* if they are set in motion by God. Otherwise they are dead works and will be burned up at the Bema seat judgement. This has left Pastors exhausted and Church members living with guilt for not performing or reaching 'quotas'. God does not want this. He is responsible for the growth of His Church and all we have to do is listen for His guidance. So many Church programmes today are humanistic and often fail, leading to apathy and disinterest in congregants. It never ceases to amaze me that Jesus chastised Martha for working around Him, fussing over this and that while Mary sat at His feet and drank from the depth of the experience. God wants *relationships,* he wants your heart and not your programmes, unless of course He inspired them. We all know what it's like to have a husband or wife that is so busy you cannot talk to them. God feels the same way, He came to give us (mental and spiritual) rest.

Humanism has allowed homosexuality, transgender and same sex marriage to creep in, mainly because political correctness has crushed free speech and the silent majority bow their heads in despair but do nothing about it. What did Jesus do when He saw the money-changers in the temples? He smashed their tables and threw their coins all over the place. Modern Christianity has made Jesus look like an effeminate wimp and that character has slumped over the shoulders of believers, coupled with society's planned sidelining of the male does not foster well for the power and strength of the Church in the last days.

In order to delay the 'Day of the Lord' in congregants minds 'Pastors' now teach Preterism, the false doctrine that all prophetic scripture except the return of Christ was fulfilled when Rome crushed Israel in AD 70. This gives believers a sort of 'stay of execution' for being responsible for anything if the Lord's return is far in the future, if ever. Some sects even believe Jesus has already returned (with the mess the world is in!).

Others foolishly believe the Church has taken on the promises God gave to the Jews and that they are now a spent force. That is why some mainstream Churches support divesting from Israel. 'They' killed Jesus so they deserve to be cut off. This is the false doctrine of 'replacement theology'.

And finally, others believe we are building a great Church for Jesus to return to and become Head of. How this Church will survive the Great Tribulation and all the earthquakes and wars is anyone's guess. This is called 'Kingdom now' theology. Please turn from this belief if you are one of its members.

The Luciferian Doctrine, Technology, UFOs and other nasties

As mentioned in the main body of this work the Luciferian Doctrine will play an absolutely massive role in people being destroyed by God in the final days of the Wrath that He visits upon Earth. This is a doctrine, surprisingly well supported, that Lucifer is God and God is the Devil. It is supported (perhaps unknowingly by some of its members) in Masonic lodges the world over as well as by witches and literally dozens of cults and false religions. Lucifer means 'Light bearer' which is seen as light with God being dark and sinister.

New-age adherents believe:- (1) All is one, all reality is part of the whole; (2) Everything is God and God is everything; (3) Man is God or a part of God; (4) Man never dies, but continues to live through reincarnation; (5) Man can create his own reality and/or values through transformed consciousness or altered states of consciousness. It's this group that poses a massive threat to the Tribulation Saints in the last days as they believe we have reached a point in time where we need to 'jump' to our next point in evolution. This is a group, along with many others that believe science, 'god' and humans must all come together as one to move forward. (Perhaps this is why the CEOs of several multi-billion dollar organizations have said that Artificial Intelligence is the biggest threat to mankind). The three evil spirits Satan sends out to deceive people in the last days will convince these willing participants that the Antichrist is the god-particle they have been waiting for. I believe many of the miracles the Antichrist and False Prophet perform will be counterfeit, perhaps resting on technology like Project Blue beam (holograms) and demonic acts in the skies above us, bringing down fire and so on.

I also believe that lying signs and wonders will be used to explain the rapture away, that Christians were 'removed' as they are the bad guys and now humanity can take the next leap forward in its 'evolution' which in itself is another Satanic lie. It's possible that some type of demonic UFO signs or a message from above will convince many to follow the Beast when he arrives while also convincing many others that the 'crazy' Christians who used to witness to them were actually right all along and it's time to follow Christ.

My next book will be on the occult/technology combination that scientists want to integrate into mankind as a tool to make us better, stronger but ultimately more subservient. My interest started when I read the report of the first military man to reach the Roswell crash site in 1947. He stated that the only survivor spoke telepathically with him through a stone on its forehead. This immediately made me think of Revelation 13:16 that all humans must have a mark on their foreheads under the Antichrist. The person who related this story went on to talk about the Ariel School UFO landing in Zimbabwe in 1994 where all the children at school witnessed a UFO land and small people get out. The terrified children were all interviewed separately and gave pretty much the same story which is almost impossible, so it must have been a true sighting. This led to the researcher, who I personally met in Harare, stating that when he left the Ariel site he walked into the bush and met some local Africans who told him that they often see these small beings at night. They showed him carvings they had made of a small being with a big head and slanted eyes and a stone on its forehead. In further travels to Botswana the Bushmen told him they were common, along with orbs of light (light-bearers) that visited at night and indeed while he was there he saw them. The Bushmen also made carvings and they too were of beings with big heads and slanted eyes and a stone or mark or symbol on their foreheads.

I the author have now collected dozens of photographs of masks made by primitive tribes all over the world and many, many of them show beings with a big head, slanted eyes and something on the forehead.

What has this got to do with the End Times?

Well, I believe that a massive part of the Luciferian Doctrine is made up with demonic beings posing as bringers of light (Lucifer) who will encourage telepathic thinking and communication through the 'mark' attached to unsaved peoples' foreheads. This device will control these people and make them subservient to the Antichrist and is probably why they will attack God's armies in the battle of Armageddon so willingly. We have all seen pictures of third eyes in foreheads and triangles situated there and so on. This is where man thinks and processes information, in the frontal lobe. The mark in the wrist will be for banking and other records of the bearer of that mark. Tribulation Saints who reject all of this technology will be cut out of the buying and selling system of the Antichrist as stated in Revelation 13:17. Remember, the unsaved will be *so convinced* that Lucifer is God that they will *willingly* go to war for him.

Final say

My dear friends, the scenario outlined in this book, at least the bit about the return of Christ, *will definitely happen*. You may therefore ask how you can be saved from the terror of not knowing Jesus in the last hour. It is quite simple. Accept Him as your saviour by simply saying with your mouth, 'Dear Lord Jesus, I accept you as my Saviour and repent of all the sins I have committed in my life. Please forgive me and accept me into your Kingdom'. If you have done that with sincerity in your heart, you are saved and I can call you brother or sister and you now dwell in the Kingdom of Light. Come Lord Jesus come.

See you in the clouds!

Lightning Source UK Ltd.
Milton Keynes UK
UKHW041816131218

333940UK00002B/145/P

9 781527 233072